T0149721

THE PSYCHOLOGY OF HOPE

KEYS TO GREATER HAPPINESS AND SUCCESS

G. A. MOHR
R. S. MOHR
& P. E. MOHR

THE PSYCHOLOGY OF HOPE
KEYS TO GREATER HAPPINESS
AND SUCCESS

G. A. Mohr
R. S. Mohr
& P. E. Mohr

BALBOA.
PRESS
A DIVISION OF HAY HOUSE

Balboa Press books may be ordered through booksellers or by contacting:

Balboa Press
A Division of Hay House
1663 Liberty Drive
Bloomington, IN 47403
www.balboapress.com.au
1 (877) 407-4847

Print information available on the last page.

ISBN: 978-1-5043-1221-9 (sc)
ISBN: 978-1-5043-1222-6 (e)

Balboa Press rev. date: 01/22/2018

ALSO BY G. A. MOHR

A Microcomputer Introduction to the Finite Element Method
A Treatise on the Finite Element Method
Finite Elements for Solids, Fluids, and Optimization
The MBS: A Course in Management Science
Finite Elements and Optimization for Modern Management
Natural Finite Elements Using Basis Transformation
The Pretentious Persuaders,
A Brief History & Science of Mass Persuasion

Curing Cancer & Heart Disease,
Proven Ways to Combat Aging, Atherosclerosis & Cancer

The Variant Virus, Introducing Secret Agent Simon Sinclair
The Doomsday Calculation, The End Of The Human Race
The War of the Sexes, Women Are Getting On Top
Heart Disease, Cancer, & Ageing:
Proven Neutraceutical & Lifestyle Solutions

2045: A Remote Town Survives Global Holocaust
The History & Psychology of Human Conflict
Elementary Thinking for the 21st Century
The 8-Week+ Program to Reverse Cardiovascular Disease
The Scientific MBA

ALSO WITH R.S. MOHR (ALIAS RICHARD SINCLAIR) & P.E. MOHR (ALIAS EDWIN FEAR):

The Evolving Universe: Relativity, Redshift and Life from Space
(with Richard Sinclair & Edwin Fear)
World Religions: The History, Psychology, Issues & Truth
(with Edwin Fear)
World War 3, When & How Will It End?
(with Edwin Fear & Richard Sinclair)
The Brainwashed, From Consumer Zombies to Islamic Jihad
(with Edwin Fear)
Human Intelligence, Learning & Behaviour
(with Richard Sinclair & Edwin Fear)

THE PSYCHOLOGY OF HOPE

TABLE OF CONTENTS

PREFACE

Having written such books as *The Pretentious Persuaders, World Religions, The Brainwashed,* and *Human Intelligence, Learning & Behaviour,* about how religious, political and corporate advertising reduce us to "consumer zombies", and in other books such as *The Doomsday Calculation, The History & Psychology of Human Conflicts,* and *World War 3,* lamented that overpopulation, resource depletion, pollution, evolution of new diseases, and increasingly widespread and sophisticated nuclear and biochemical weapons threaten our very survival as a species, a book on HOPE is perhaps both worthwhile and timely.

The motivation for this came in part from noticing that, in some of the aforementioned books, I had concluded that we should HOPE to solve the many and growing problems that face mankind, suggesting, for example, that *real democracy* is badly needed around the world, rather than dictatorships, military juntas, and oligarchical governments that now govern almost the entire world.

Then, of course, we need to have sensible goals and plans to achieve them, for example, to limit human population growth, and ultimately reduce the global human population. In that way only, perhaps, can we deal with such issues as resource depletion, pollution and global warming in the long term.

So the authors HOPE that some of the ideas in this book help not only improve the lives of individuals, but also motivate them to improve the world we live in, and thence the lives of others.

Geoff Mohr, 2018

CHAPTER 1

INTRODUCTION

Twenty-five hundred years ago it might have been said that man understood himself as well as any other part of this world. Today he is the thing he understands least. Physics and biology have come a long way, but there has been no comparable development of anything like a science of human behaviour.
B. F. Skinner, q. in *50 Psychology Classics,* T. Butler-Bowdon, 2017.

Evolution of tribal man

Humans evolved from animal origins and thus possess the same physical and behavioural characteristics as most of the larger land-based animal species. Physically, we eat, we sleep, we defecate, and so forth.

What sets us apart, however, is an enlarged cerebral cortex which stores the semantic memory needed for the advanced languages that we take so long to learn in infancy.

Chimpanzees, with which we share circa 96% of the same genes, are sociable animals that live in groups of 20 to 60, forming into subgroups of adults (male and female), all-male groups, and groups of mothers and offspring. African gorillas also live in bisexual groups of between 2 to 30 but which do not comprise smaller subgroups.

The best known studies of chimpanzees were conducted by Jane Goodall and associates in the Gombe National Park on the edge of Lake Tanganyika in Tanzania (Goodall, 1971). Ultimately, Goodall was disillusioned to find that *tribes* of chimps were led by an alpha male and would occasionally have small wars with neighbouring tribes, these resuming at intervals over periods of many years. She concluded that they were all too much like humans!

1

1. INTRODUCTION

Comparisons of blood proteins and the DNA of the African great apes with that of humans indicates that the line leading to modern people did not split off from that of chimpanzees and gorillas until comparatively late in evolution, perhaps 6 million to 8 million years ago.

Fossils of the first *hominines,* the *australopithecines,* dating to 5 million years ago have been discovered. This genus seems to have become extinct about 1.5 million years ago, but before doing so one of seven species of australopithecines, *Australopithecus africanus,* evolved into the genus *Homo* between 1.5 and 2 million years ago.

The earliest evidence of stone tools comes from sites in Africa dated to about 2.5 million years ago. These tools seem to be associated with all hominine species.

Around 1.7 to 1.9 million years ago two new species of large brained, small-toothed hominines emerged, *Homo ergaster* in Africa and *Homo erectus* in Asia. Later *H. erectus* skulls possess brain sizes in the range of 1100 to 1300 cc (67.1 to 79.3 cu in), within the size variation of *Homo sapiens.*

A number of archaeological sites dating from the time of *Homo erectus* reveal a greater sophistication in tool-making than was found at earlier sites. Evidence found at the cave site of "Peking Man" in northern China, suggests that *Homo erectus* used fire.

The remains of the foundations of an oval structure built by a *Homo erectus* group were found at the Terra-Amata site in France, and within this structure, there was a fireplace (Weiss and Mann, 1978).

The *Homo* species spread widely and by 350,000 years ago planned hunting, fire making, wearing of clothes, and probably burial rituals, were well established.

Between 200,000 and 300,000 years ago, *Homo sapiens* evolved. The Neanderthals or *Homo sapiens neanderthalensis* had similar DNA to modern man and occupied parts of Europe and the Middle East as early as 120,000 years ago. They lived only in family groups, the men being hunter-gatherers to feed the family.

1. Introduction

The Neanderthals left cave paintings that were an important evolutionary advance. These often depicted a simple activity, perhaps a precursor to the highly pictorial hieroglyphic script of the ancient Egyptians (Egerton-Eastwick, 1896).

Though Neanderthals had 10% larger brains than modern man, there is some evidence that the part of the cerebral cortex devoted to language and thinking in modern man was underdeveloped.

Thought by some to be a different evolutionary branch, the Neanderthals disappeared from the fossil record about 30,000 years ago.

Differing in appearance, modern humans or *Homo sapiens sapiens* evolved in southern Africa or the Middle East perhaps 90,000 to 200,000 years ago and 70,000 years ago began to spread to all parts of the world, reaching Europe about 40,000 years ago, soon outnumbering, perhaps interbreeding with, and finally supplanting the local, earlier *Homo sapiens* populations.

Like chimpanzees, Homo sapiens sapiens formed tribes and there is evidence of religion, recorded events and art dating from 30,000 to 40,000 years ago implying the advanced language and ethics required for the ordering of social groups.

Conflict

No doubt there was occasional conflict within the family groups that Homo sapiens lived in, perhaps, for example, over decisions about where to search and hunt for food.

Indeed, such arguments may have led to conflict over who leadership of the group should be trusted to.

There may, of course, have also been occasional conflict with other family groups over territorial issues or, in effect, 'hunting and searching rights' in certain areas which more than one group lived near.

Once tribes were established, questions of leadership may have become more important. No doubt the stronger males were likely to be chosen as leaders in both regular hunting and occasional conflicts between neighbouring tribes.

Indeed, tribal conflicts are 'war' and, of course, some American Indians still ceremonially perpetuate the practice of covering their faces with 'war paint' that traditionally preceded a tribal conflict.

In addition, the elders would often have had at least some influence, whilst their role in passing on tribal folklore would certainly have involved tales of conflicts past with other tribes, and thus encouraged acceptance and continuance of such conflicts.

In addition, tribal witch doctors or shamans would have had considerable influence, their superstitious view of things no doubt causing other tribes to be considered 'heathen' and viewed with suspicion, if not hostility.

Thus religious leaders increased the 'differences' between their tribe and others, an important factor in ethnic conflict which is further discussed in Chapter 11.

Indeed, it was often supposed that the Neanderthals were wiped out by invading Homo sapiens sapiens from the South, but is now believed that, in fact, the two closely related species interbred and thus those of us with European lineage have some Neanderthal DNA.

No doubt the invaders also killed a great many Neanderthals as well, perhaps mostly the more threatening males. In other words, in war kill the men and rape the women, something that has not changed since then in the brutality of war.

Evolution of religion

Around the same time Homo sapiens developed cave art, about 100,000 years ago, he would have developed language and, eventually some form of 'pictorial' communication which eventually evolved into hieroglyphic script, then cuneiform script, and finally the symbolic writing we now use.

Typically, each tribe had a leader, a religion, and a common language and culture.

The first forms of religion involved such beliefs and practices as:

(a) *Animism*, belief that plants, inanimate objects and natural phenomena had souls or spirits.

(b) *Polytheism*, belief in multiple Gods, sometimes attributing certain acts of nature to each.

(c) *Ancestor Worship* teaching that a tribe's people were descended from a common ancestor.

(d) *Immortality* or belief that the dead live on as spirits, promises of immortality to the faithful still being amongst the 'blackmail' tactics preachers use today.

Eventually these religions evolved into the *monotheism* that dominates the world today.

Thus, at the outset it was the tribal elders who passed on tribal beliefs from one generation to another, a situation that still exists amongst a few primitive people today. Along the way *shamans* or 'witch doctors' claiming some special connection with the spirits appeared, along with religious rites and ceremonies.

In groups of hunter-gatherers, just as with many other species of animals, the 'dominant' males were, of course, responsible for protection of the group from external threats which, just as with chimpanzees, often took the form of other 'tribes' or groups.

At the same time, however, the supposedly wiser elders still indoctrinated the young into religion and had considerable influence, if not control, over the 'dominant males.' Their weapons for control ranged from rhetoric to dire threats of a vengeful spirit or God.

Thus, from the ancient Greeks through to the middle ages a study of *rhetoric* was considered important because of its use to bullshit people into doing as political and religious leaders wished. Francis Bacon (1561 - 1626), for example, studied Elizabethan logic and rhetoric at Cambridge University for two years, leaving at the age of 14 (note that people got married at this sort of age then).

Hope

Since early in mankind's sorry history, religious BS has tended to increase man's tribalism, and thus lead to conflict, never more so than at present during a period when World War 3, that is, rampant Islamic jihad and terrorism raging throughout the world, is in full swing (Mohr, Sinclair, and Fear, 2015).

Religions, however, also promise to give people hope of a better life and eternal life in heaven after death if they obey the demands of whichever religion is the "flavour of the century" in a particular community, principal amongst those commands being to do as told by religious leaders (citing their commands as coming from some God or other), and to support and give money to the religious establishment.

Similarly, those of us who believe in love, seek out a supposedly loving partner with whom to spend our lives, hoping that this will ensure happiness, and perhaps success also.

Children, on the other hand, hope for such things as better marks at school, for example, but above all, for nice presents on their birthday anniversaries and at Christmas. The first author, however, believes that it would be nicer to give children a nice present every week to brighten their restricted and somewhat imprisoned lives, but poor people cannot, of course, afford to do so.

Adults, however, hope for such things as higher pay, a better job, or to be able to achieve some goal such as publish a book or start a business.

People with serious illnesses, on the other hand, simply hope for their health to improve, and often such hopes play an important part in recovery when this does occur.

Mindset

Psychologist Carol Dweck in her 2006 book *Mindset: The New Psychology of Success,* made the important distinction between:

(a) *Fixed mindset* which focuses heavily upon outcome: "If you fail – or if you're not the best – it's all been wasted."

(b) *Growth mindset* which focuses more upon the effort and what might have been learnt from it.

According to Butler-Bowdon some fixed mindset people allow a poor result in a single test, such as for IQ, to limit their ambitions and efforts for the rest of their lives (Butler-Bowden, 2017).

Growth mindset people, on the other hand, think much more positively and aim for new and higher goals with the view that, no matter what the outcome, they will at least have tried or 'given it a go', and can learn from the effort and thus hope to do better next time.

In a study of university students, Dweck found that those with fixed mindsets had higher levels of depression and were more likely to give up when their results were poor. Students with a growth mindset with poor results, however, took the more positive view that they had made some progress, and increased their efforts in order to obtain better results.

She therefore argues that in dealing with children we should praise the work that a child has put into a task, and the skills that they will have acquired, saying:

If they fail, explain that if they want to do better they will have to work harder. Give honest and constructive feedback, not just say things to make them feel good. Expect a lot from them, but in a warm, non-judgemental way.

7

Conclusion

In psychology hope is important, if not extremely so.

This is in part because, when we are in a positive emotional state, neurochemicals called endorphins which have analgesic properties, are released which help us overcome difficult situations.

From our schooldays, when we hope for better marks or to do well at extra-curricular activities, to adult life when we hope for a better job, a pay rise, etcetera, it is important, if not necessary, to have hope throughout life.

In Australia, at least, sporting stars use the word *"hopefully"* when interviewed about their performance and prospects of success to an extent that is almost comical, no doubt because their coaches work hard to instil in them an optimistic attitude.

The 'growth' and 'fixed' mindsets discussed in the preceding section respectively bear some comparison to the basic psychological domains of introversion and extroversion, a positive or growth mindset making people more optimistic and inclined to take on new goals with the view that, no matter what the outcome, they will learn from their efforts and can thus hope to do better next time.

Following chapters discuss the importance of hope at various stages of life, how it can improve our quality of life, help us become more successful in life and love, and how to deal with the many problems that may confront us throughout life, ranging from financial problems to physical and psychological disorders, addictions, etcetera.

Other chapters are devoted to discussing ways of treating addictions and psychological problems, such as Cognitive Behavioural Therapy (CBT), how to plan for a successful life, and how to deal with people to smooth the road to success and happiness.

Chapter 2

Growing Up With Hope

Children also need something to hope for - - big or small - - as long as it teaches them to look forward with positive expectation.
Shane J. Lopez, *Making Hope Happen* (2013).

The early years

Piaget borrowed from psychoanalysis to define two types of thought (Gillespie, 2017):

> ➤ *Directed or intelligent thought* is based on experience and logic and has realistic and communicable goals.
> ➤ *Undirected or autistic thought* via images, myths and symbols aimed at satisfying unconscious and unrealistic desires.

The directed mind sees objects as having certain properties and obeying certain laws, whereas for the autistic mind objects are simply there to be seen or enjoyed.

Piaget felt that children from 3 to 7 are largely egocentric and indulge in autistic thought, whereas from 7 to 11 they begin to develop the perceptual intelligence of the adult mind.

The formative years

The period from age 12 to 30 has been termed the *critical period* for formation of attitudes and it can be divided into two parts (Morgan et al., 1979):

(a) Adolescence, during which parental, educational, peer group, advertising and sociological influences are largely responsible for development of most of the attitudes a person will form through life.

(b) Young adulthood is a time when commitments such as choosing a vocation and marriage occur, and one in which attitudes tend to *crystallize* or 'freeze' for life.

In part this crystallization may involve attempts at *cognitive consistency* in which we tend to make our attitudes relatively consistent with one another and thus avoid *cognitive dissonance* or conflicting attitudes.

Heider's *balance theory* is of the cognitive consistency type and assumes that we try to maintain consistent and balanced or harmonious relationships with other people and our environment. According to this theory we would not marry a person with whom we disagreed on major issues about which we felt strongly, such as abortion (Morgan et al., 1979).

That attitudes do indeed crystallize or 'firm up' in young adulthood was confirmed by a US survey of women college students in the 1930s which, when followed-up 20 years later, found that for most issues on the 'conservative-liberal' dimension the women's attitudes, except for a slight "conservative drift" typical of older people, remained the same as they had been in their twenties (Newcomb, 1963).

That attitudes tend to firm up in adolescence and young adulthood has, of course, important implication for how we are likely to live the rest of our lives.

Preschool education

Children's brains develop rapidly in the first few years and it is important to take advantage of their resulting capacity for early learning to provide infants with a stimulating environment which should include a 'personal learning centre' that includes educational pictures and toys.

By the second year they should be involved in small learning groups supervised by a specialist teacher so that they can begin real learning (Packard, 1978).

In the third year they should begin kindergarten for at least a couple of days a week and these learning efforts should continue. By now they have a modest vocabulary and are capable of *cognitive learning* which processes and stores *abstract* information.

At this stage deliberate effort should be made at 'IQ building', noting that IQ tests include questions testing verbal, spatial and numerical ability. If a child has a problem with numbers, for example, early detection and correction of this will prevent far greater problems later.

Then, given a head start, they should commence school at age four, rather than the usual five in most countries.

Home schooling

In the USA home schooling has increased markedly in recent decades. The number of home-schooled children grew from just a few thousand in the early 1970s to 1.1 million in 2003, having increased 30% between 1999 and 2003 (Penn, 2007).

In 2000, only 52 percent of colleges had formal admission policies for home-schooled students, but by 2005 85% did, in that year a study showing that home-schooled students scored 81 points higher than the national average on the SAT (Penn, 2007).

Enhancing the learning process

The home learning process can be enhanced by such means as the 'Superlearning' recommended by Ostrander and Schroeder (1979). This involves encouraging physical and psychological relaxation with quite background music, slow breathing exercises, and visualizing nice scenes to achieve a reflective and receptive frame of mind.

Then the child is encouraged to affirm: *"I can do it."*

Here, developing a positive attitude is comparable to the 'teacher expectancy effect' where it is found that students who already get good marks are encouraged to do even better by a combination of the positive results, the confidence they obtain from these, and the 'expectation' and confidence the teacher shows about their ability. Here *hope* plays an important part, and students who become accustomed to getting low marks tend to lose hope, and without hope, of course, life is much less bearable.

With the scene set, the parent/teacher reads the material aloud at a careful pace while the child reads it silently. This is repeated again with quiet background music and the child is then tested on the material.

Motivation

Aristotle was first to assert that our goal was to become more nearly what we were intended to be. Psychologists refer to this is as *self-actualization* and Maslow viewed this as striving to reach our potential (Lindzey at al., 1978). He defined two kinds of needs:

(a) *Basic needs* such as hunger, thirst, sex and security.

(b) *Metaneeds* such as achievement, beauty, goodness, justice, order and unity.

Maslow defined achievement as a basic need but the present authors prefer to classify it as a 'higher' or more human metaneed.

First, we must meet our basic or 'animal' needs. That done, we can turn our attention to the higher 'human' metaneeds, and thence self-actualization as a human being.

These needs provide *primary goals* that may motivate us towards *secondary goals* such as money in order to achieve them.

Most of our basic needs are *intrinsic motivations*. Of these, *competence motivation* is perhaps the most basic and is learnt by infants challenged by goals such as standing up in their cot or walking.

Most of our metaneeds are *learned goals.* Achievement motivation, for example, can be inculcated by parents or teachers. *Social motivations* such as justice are also acquired in this way.

What has this got to do with thinking? One's motivations will, of course, greatly influence how one thinks and acts.

Some studies have found, however, little correlation between motivation and efficiency of learning, suggesting that genetics and practice are more important factors.

Giving children more attention and hope

Weiss and Mann (1978) refer to a project in Milwaukee that found that children given more attention by the mother or a specially trained teacher, showed markedly higher IQ. This is no doubt the reason that only children tend to have higher IQ and that, in families with more than one child, the eldest child has a slightly higher IQ on average (Vernon, 1960). The youngest child in larger families, on the other hand, does not do too badly compared to those 'sandwiched' in the middle and perhaps most deprived of attention.

Related to this, of course, is the 'teacher expectancy effect, in which students who get better marks are not only themselves encouraged by getting good results, but also by teachers often openly predicting that they will continue to do well.

As Lopez (2013) puts it:

Children also need something to hope for. They need to be excited about one thing in the future . . . then another, then another.

As Marta (2004) puts it:

Each of us has a responsibility to have a positive impact on the children we know.

Talk about the future – their dreams and aspirations – throughout their lives, not just at important milestones.

Goal setting

As with the teacher expectancy effect, goal setting and positive thinking play an important role in many other activities in life. In sports, for example, coaches do their utmost to encourage positive thinking and goal setting, and much psychological research has been done in this area, Sykes (1995) citing several examples of doctorates in education being granted for dissertations with such titles as:

"The use of goal setting and positive self-modelling to enhance self-efficiency and performance for the basketball free-throw shot" for a PhD at the University of Maryland.

Preferably, however, goals should not be 'commanded'. Rather, they should be 'suggested' and should be personal goals, not 'institutional' ones.

Conclusions

According to Lopez (2013):

Optimism is partly based on temperament – some babies come into the world inclined to embrace experience, while others shy away. The components of hopeful thinking are learned in early childhood; if all goes well, they're in place by age two.

Thus, both because of the rapid rate at which neural connections are made in the brain in the first years of life, (Mohr 2012a, 2014c), and because the very young brain is more open and receptive, the formative years are crucial, and efficient, personal, and encouraging early learning can increase a child's IQ substantially (Mohr, 2012d).

In addition, children who are brought up with positive thinking, goal setting, and encouragement are likely to have better, more successful, and happier lives.

CHAPTER 3

RELIGION

Where questions of religion are concerned,
people are guilty of every possible sort of
dishonesty and intellectual misdemeanour.
Sigmund Freud, *The Future of an Illusion* (1927), ch. 6.

Looking for meaning

Concentration camp survivor Viktor Frankl's form of existential psychology, "logotherapy", proposes that humans are uniquely made to seek meaning in life, even in the worst of times, and no matter how bad the circumstances, we are always left with some degree of free will.

Eric Hoffer wrote in *The True Believer* that "people allow themselves to be swept up in the larger causes in order to be freed of responsibility for their own lives, and to escape the banality and misery of the present (Butler-Bowden, 2017).

Hoffer's view applies very well, of course, to religion, mankind having been duped into following countless religions throughout history.

Ignorance, Fables and Lies

From the outset religions involved ignorance and superstition as primitive man developed language and applied it to the bewildering array of objects he found surrounding him to name spirits that control most things in nature, including man himself.

Though slowly at first, our understanding of the world grew with time. After all, the first author's grandmother was born only 11 years after Darwin published his theory of evolution.

Since that time the industrial revolution, and the scientific revolution that underpinned it, have accelerated greatly.

Corruption and dishonesty began to appear in religions with the appearance of shamans claiming communication with spirits and using the same sorts of tricks that magicians use today to fool their audiences (Clark, 2012). This was, perhaps, the original example of the saying 'power corrupts' which is epitomized in the quotation that opens this chapter.

Then, of course, as communities grew, so too did the power of religious and community leaders. As monarchs appeared, they usually chose to identify with, and often assume leadership of a particular religion. Indeed, sometimes they went so far as to have themselves declared gods, as did Roman emperor Julius Caesar in 42BC.

This event, no doubt, encouraged the Jews to quickly find a new messiah to free the Holy City of Jerusalem from the Roman rule that had been established by Pompey in 63BC.

That Jesus had been born out of wedlock probably gave his mother and her relatives the idea of pronouncing him the son of God, which a 'voice from heaven' is supposed to have done when John the Baptist, Mary's cousin, baptized him when he was circa 30.

Then Jesus supposedly spent 40 days in the wilderness, resisting temptation by the devil three times, after which he found his first four disciples by the Sea of Galilee. The great hoax of his crucifixion, however, was perhaps the greatest scams of all time, as briefly detailed in Chapter 17, one which led to Christianity spreading around the world, initially with the help of Jesus and some of his original disciples, even being adopted by Rome after a few hundred years.

Such fables of visions and voices from God occur again and again as giving yet another 'religion starter' the status of prophet, further examples being (some dates approximate):

➢ 1300 BC: Moses commanded by God to lead the Hebrews, and his communications with God atop Mount Sinai.

➢ 620 BC: Zoroaster's vision of Ahura Mazda (creator God), the basis of Zoroastrianism or Mazdaism.

> ➢ 440 BC: Buddha's visions while sitting under a tree.
> ➢ 610: Muhammad's command from heaven "Recite!"
> ➢ 1496: Guru Nanek's (founder of Sikhism) visions.
> ➢ 1744: Swedenborg's religion-founding visions.
> ➢ 1827: Joseph Smith's (founder of Mormonism) visions.
> ➢ 1852: Baha Ullah's (founder of Baha'i) visions.
> ➢ 1930: Wallace Fard's (founder of Nation of Islam) visions.

As with Jesus, in the case of Moses there was a political motive for his visions, namely to lead the Hebrews out of captivity in Egypt.

In the case of Muhammad there may also have been a political motive (Encarta Encyclopedia 1999):

Muhammad probably heard Christians and Jews expound their religious views at commercial fairs in Mecca, and, troubled by the questions they raised, he periodically withdrew to a cave outside Mecca to meditate and pray for guidance. During one of these retreats he experienced a vision of the archangel Gabriel, who proclaimed him a prophet of God.

His motive, of course, is similar to that which Jesus had, namely to proclaim a new religion which would help conquer his 'holy city', Mecca, exactly what he and his followers did in 1630. Then, as with Christianity, the Muslim faith was spread widely, much conflict often being used to subdue other religions.

That so many people would follow religions is understandable in primitive times when there was not much else to do in one's spare time. After all, the world's first printed book only appeared in 868, this being the *Diamond Sutra,* a translation of a short Buddhist script. Before then, of course, scriveners laboured hard in monasteries to produce a few copies of religious texts such as the Bible, these being used by priests to brainwash the public. Then, just as children believe fairy tales, ancient people believed religious fables.

Circa 2000BC the Babylonians had knowledge of the Pythagorean Theorem and solved quadratic equations. Pythagoras (c.580 – 500BC) and scholars of that period, however, postulated a spherical earth moving in a circular orbit about a central fire. It was not until 1984, however, that the Vatican declared that the inquisition had been incorrect in convicting Galileo of heresy in 1632 for supporting the Copernican view of the universe.

So it is that religion still fills ignorant men's minds with superstition and prejudice, leading to results such as the two centuries of conflict during the Reformation, and the ongoing conflict between Sunni and Shiite Muslims in the world today.

Proliferation of New Religions & Sects

The manner in which new religions and sects have proliferated in the last 2500 years is more astounding than any particular religious creed itself. The Axial Age (800 – 200BC) is so called because it saw great changes in culture and religion with the appearance of Zoroastrianism, Buddhism, Taoism, Confucianism, and the great Hebrew prophets of the 6th century BC (Jeremiah, Ezekiel, and the unknown author of Isaiah 40-66) in the space of about 200 years (620BC +).

Many religions have been created since, including several in the last century.

In addition, countless new religious sects have been created since 1500, particularly of Christianity, but also of Islam and Hinduism.

Often, of course, a religious story grows with time. Thus primitive polytheistic religions would have begun with few spirits or gods and added many more over time. Some of these religions, however, such as that of a few primitive tribes in New Guinea, had a supreme god.

Not surprisingly, therefore, monotheism took root, particularly in Judaism, spreading greatly thanks to a proliferation of prophets, particularly Jesus and Muhammad.

Then, however, various schisms occurred in Christianity as people sought independence from the central powers of the Pope in Rome. The greatest of these was the Reformation which ultimately, after a great deal of conflict, saw the establishment of several Protestant movements, most of which survive to this day.

Similarly, there was a great divide amongst Muslims between the Sunnis and Shiites which began in 680AD, and which causes conflict to this day. Since then several other sects have been established, including the Sufis, the Wahhabis, and Nation of Islam.

The Hare Krishna Hindu sect is an excellent example of a new religious sect, being begun by the penniless founder sitting in the streets and chanting 'Hare Krishna.'

As noted earlier, Christianity and Islam were probably created for political reasons, and were ultimately successful in that regard, being the basis for a great deal of religious imperialism that saw these religions overtake numerous countries around the world.

Relatively recent examples of politically motivated religions or sects include the Maori Ratana Church, Rastafarianism and Nation of Islam, all of these seeking some degree of freedom of black peoples from repression.

Other religions were created as an exercise akin to writing a novel or play, but with full knowledge that, as history had long shown, religion could bring a great deal of influence, power and money, as the massive temples built for various religions have demonstrated vividly for millennia.

There are several examples of this throughout history in which a person, sometimes from a privileged background, became discontented and changed lifestyle dramatically, then claimed to have seen a vision but, of course, without any witnesses to this moment of epiphany. Then, of course, given a few disciples, a new religion can be spread, in ancient times only to be recorded in writing after centuries of rumour had embellished the original fables greatly.

Needless to say, of course, the many scriveners who recorded and then copied religious texts were paid for their efforts by way of food and lodging in monasteries.

Similarly, preachers are, however, paid for their efforts and, indeed, becoming a priest was only a couple of centuries ago in Europe one of relatively few occupations an educated person could aspire to, religious education dominating higher education in Europe until the 12th century and beyond.

In more modern times, of course, the money motive became more obvious, the farcical circumstances of the foundation of the Mormon Church being just one of many examples (Mohr & Fear, 2014).

In Chapter 17 the new religion of Mohronism is discussed, and this, hopefully, will prove successful before long.

Religious Corruption

In ancient times 'religion starters' did so for political reasons, Moses, Christ and Muhammad being notable examples, in each case their real cause being escaping domination by another culture. More recent examples are the Maori Ratana Church, Rastafarianism, and Nation of Islam.

Religion is also, of course, big business, and many a self-proclaimed prophet starting a new religion was well aware of this.

People spruiking a religion, whether new or old, are selling a product of sorts, so why is this corrupt?

The answer is that they are selling a pack of fables and lies sold as truth. The sheer multiplicity of religions is testament to the implicit dishonesty of religion itself, the endless arguments and conflicts about sometimes minor differences between religions being convincing evidence that, in the end, all religions are telling lies for the most part.

3. RELIGION

The more contemplative religions such as Confucianism or Buddhism, which place less emphasis on dogma about some god or other and countless rules, are perhaps less dishonest, and historically they seem to have caused much less harm in the way of conflict and terrorism.

Sometimes people who started religions came from a well-to-do background from which they might have learnt the sort of dishonesty required to extract money from gullible people, examples being Confucius and Buddha.

In other cases they were poverty stricken people, for example A.C. Bhaktivedanta, the founder of the Hare Krishna movement, who arrived in New York with only $50 and began chanting on a sidewalk, the small trickle of money that brought no doubt turning into a flood as the movement grew.

Such religious founders as Joseph Smith (Mormonism) and Ron Hubbard (Scientology) were also obviously bent on making money, as the brief details of how they founded religions given in Chapters 9 and 10 of the book *World Religions* (Mohr & Fear, 2014) illustrate.

Another example was Oral Roberts, a Pentecostal preacher who in the 1950s reached wide audiences through radio and television. He founded a publishing company and Oral Roberts University in Tulsa, from which he retired as president in the early 1990s, having become known for his luxurious way of life.

A further example was the conviction in 1988 of popular television evangelist Jim Bakker for fraud.

Indeed, when all is said and done, the business of religion is to make money and religious organizations cannot survive without it. Today, many major religions are fabulously wealthy, having landholdings around the world of incalculable value and on which they are usually exempt from taxes.

Indeed, the excessive power and wealth of the Roman Catholic Church was a major factor in the discontent that sparked the Reformation in Europe.

Similarly, taxation inequalities in Muslim countries have often been a cause of conflict.

The excessive power and wealth of the Catholic Church in France, and its association with the aristocracy, were in part the cause of the French Revolution of 1789. The transformed society that followed confiscated the church's vast land holdings, and by 1790 religious orders had been dissolved, the remaining clergy being made elected state employees. Many priests who refused to take an oath of allegiance to the state were forbidden from preaching, and during the Reign of Terror in 1793/4 many priests were massacred.

Today the major corruption issue facing the Christian Church is that of child sexual abuse, the Catholic Church being the main offender, perhaps because of its greater number of religious schools and hostels for children. In Australia there has been outrage in recent years over disclosures that the activities of paedophile priests have been hidden from the public for decades, offending priests being discretely moved to new locations to continue preaching and offending.

Thus, according to Anne Roche Muggeridge (1986):

A miracle is certainly called for if the Catholic Church is not to disappear from places where it survived or regrouped after the Reformation, or triumphantly established itself anew in missionary territory. It has already disappeared from tens of millions of hearts which only lately were committed to it in countries where, on the surface, it still exhibits an imposing physical presence.

The major issue facing Muslim religion leaders is the need for them to speak out strongly against Islamist terrorism. Otherwise, it seems likely that daily sectarian Muslim conflict will continue for decades in several countries, particularly Iraq and Syria.

Conclusions

In 1650 Anglican bishop James Usher used the Bible to calculate that the world had been created during the night preceding October 23, 4004BC (Cooke, 2011).

Despite such absurdities, some 2 billion people are said to be Christians today, though I suspect that less than 10% of that number practice the faith to any real extent. Then, however, simply praying regularly will hardly achieve anything concrete. More nearly it is a waste of time and money, as have been the massive temples erected for countless religions for millennia. Donating money to charity might be a better course, so long as a sufficient percentage of the money found its way to the needy, that being in some doubt in some charities with extensive hierarchical structures at the top of which are executives may make unjustifiably large salaries, just as they do in other businesses.

Generally, therefore, religion makes no more sense than following a particular sporting team, and that can become akin to a religion in the case, for example, of the British Premier League. That too, however, is a waste of time and money, and one would be wiser and healthier if one exercised one's own body and brain sometimes.

As for the spate of terrorism around the world today, most of it Islamic in origin, the vengefulness of many passages of the Christian Bible, for example reference to *"the Book of the Wars of the LORD"* in Numbers 21:14, is, like much else, repeated in the Koran, for example (Dawood, 2006):

4.74: *Let those who would exchange the life of this world for the hereafter, fight for the cause of God; whoever fights for the cause of God, whether he dies or triumphs, on him We shall bestow a rich recompense.*

47.4+: *When you meet the unbelievers in the battlefield strike off their heads and, when you have laid them low, bind your captives firmly. Then grant them their freedom or take a ransom from them, until War shall lay down her burdens.*

Thus shall you do. Had God willed, He would Himself have punished them; [but He has ordained it thus] that HE may test you, the one by the other.

As for those who are slain in the cause of God, He will not allow their works to perish. He will vouchsafe them guidance and ennoble their state; He will admit them to the Paradise He has made known to them.

Here we see the invitation to conflict, and the promise of martyrdom, that has encouraged the countless suicide bombings that still occur in the Muslim world today, particularly in Iraq.

Much of that conflict is sectarian between the more fundamentalist Shiite minority and the Sunni majority, and is to some extent comparable to the many decades of conflict between Christian Protestant sects and the Roman Catholic Church that occurred during the Reformation.

Globally, little more than 10% of Muslims are Shiites, but nevertheless Shia Muslims are in the majority in Iran, Iraq, Bahrain, Azerbaijan, and perhaps Yemen. There are also large Shia communities in Afghanistan, India, Kuwait, Lebanon, Pakistan, Qatar, Syria, Turkey, Saudi Arabia and the UAE. In several of these countries considerable conflict between Shiites and Sunnis continues.

Perhaps a bottom line on key issues concerning religion today is found in the 2008 book *The God Delusion* by Richard Dawkins.

In this he talks of the "legendary" brutality which the Christian Brothers and the "sadistically cruel" Catholic nuns brought to education in Ireland.

Asked after a lecture in Dublin about reported sexual abuse by Catholic priests in Ireland, Dawkins replied along the lines that "horrible as sexual abuse no doubt was, the damage was arguably less than the long-term psychological damage inflicted by bringing a child up Catholic in the first place." He recalled that he received a round of enthusiastic applause from the audience.

As for the important issue of the false hopes that religions give to their followers, this has many unfortunate consequences, including:

1. People are conned into believing that God or some prophet will absolve all their sins, so that they can sin as much as they like and then regularly seek absolution for their sins by prayer etc.
2. People are led to believe that their lives will be made good and fulfilling if they grovel to the commands of preachers, instead of making sensible, logical plans for their lives.
3. Now matter bad how circumstances get, people are promised eternal life in a wonderful heaven, making real quality of life in the here and now seem of secondary importance.
4. Throughout history people have been persuaded to fight to spread and/or defend their religion with such absurd promises as hundreds of virgins in heaven to be given to Muslim men who die fighting for their evil religion. The result has been thousands of years of conflict around the world (Mohr & Fear, 2014; Mohr & Fear, 2016), with Islamist jihad having reached epidemic proportions around the world in recent decades (Mohr, Sinclair & Fear, 2015).

From the earliest shamans, to the newest religions, people have been duped by false prophets and crooks seeking power, influence and wealth.

Earlier the clever hoaxes involved in founding Christianity were briefly discussed, whilst Chapter 17 outlines the perhaps greatest hoax of history, the Crucifixion of Christ who most certainly did not die on the cross.

The farcical circumstances which began many other religions, including Mormonism and Scientology, are discussed in the recent book *World Religions, The History, Issues, and Truth* (Mohr & Fear, 2015).

3. RELIGION

CHAPTER 4

HOPE IMPROVES LIFE

Hope against hope, and ask till ye receive.
James Montgomery, "The World Before the Flood",
The Poetical Works of James Montgomery (1840-41).

Scientific proof

A home-based study of almost 800 people included the simple question:

Are you hopeful about the future?

Regardless of their sex or ethnicity, 91% of the respondents replied "yes", the other 9% replying "no" (Lopez, 2013).

The two groups, the "hopeful" and the "hopeless", were almost the same age (averaging respectively 69 and 70), had the same levels of education and health, with "no significant differences in blood pressure, body mass index, and drinking behaviour".

The hopeful, however, had higher levels of physical activity, fewer were smokers, tested for much lower levels of depression and higher measures of social well-being, had more social contacts, and were slightly better off financially.

About a decade later only 11% of the hopefuls had died, compared to 29% of the hopeless, the principal researcher concluding that: "If you are hopeless you are less likely to keep doctor's appointments" (Lopez, 2013).

Hope vs. optimism

The 2nd edition of the Macquarie Dictionary defines hope as: 1. expectation of something desired; desire accompanied by expectation.

2. a particular instance of such expectation or desire: *a hope of success.*

It defines optimism as:

1. disposition to hope for the best; tendency to look on the bright side of things.

while defining optimistic as:

1. disposed to take a favourable view of things.

Here optimism is a mood, a state of mind, usually without a specific goal, whereas hope is usually associated with a particular wish or ambition.

According to Lopez, however, hope is more important:

But when life throws us a curve, when the going gets tough, optimists get stuck and frustrated. Hopeful people shine in negative situations. They are energized to act and they find meaning and dignity in moving ahead, whatever the challenge.

Creating goals

Happy and successful lives are far more likely if we plan them by creating goals. These should be realistic in terms of time and resource requirements, and goals which we are enthusiastic about are, of course, more likely to receive attention and thus be achieved.

When a goal involves solving a problem it is best to think positively about it. If one is having problems with a co-worker Jim, for example, rather than think:

I want to have less trouble with Jim

it is better to think: *I want to make friends with Jim*

and act positively by, for example, paying him polite compliments occasionally.

It is also best, of course, to choose goals that your abilities are best suited to, and Chapter 14 details some systematic methods of planning for a successful life.

Leading with hope

Lopez (2013) cites a telephone Gallup poll of more than 10,000 people which asked them what three words best described how bosses or community leaders contributed positively to their life. It turned out that words such as *wisdom* were rarely mentioned, but that respondents said *"they want the people they serve to meet four psychological needs: compassion, stability, trust, and hope."*

Lopez concludes that most leaders *"do not spend enough time making hope happen"* but spend more time reacting to problems rather than planning for a better future.

The Gallup poll found that 69% of people who said their workplace leader make them enthusiastic about the future rated highly on measures of their involvement with and enthusiasm for their work. They were also more innovative, productive, and likely to stay longer with the company.

On the other hand, only 1% of those who did not find their boss made them enthusiastic about the future were committed to and enthusiastic about their work. They were also likely to be physically and mentally unhealthy, and to undermine the work of others.

Teacher expectancy effect

The teacher expectancy effect is based on the observation that students aware of the fact that the teacher considers them 'bright' tend to do better than they otherwise would, even if they are not actually exceptional. In addition, teachers tend to mark students they consider bright more favourably (perhaps we could call this 'teachers pet syndrome'). Thus we have a double barrelled effect.

For the present discussion, however, we shall merely consider an *expectancy effect* for which we write

$$Motivation = (Valence) \times (Expectancy)$$

where *valence* is the desire for marks (or in other spheres for $) and *expectancy* is the person's notion of the probability of obtaining a certain mark (perhaps enhanced by the teacher or, just as likely, by knowledge of their own record).

This expectancy is of a first level outcome (obtaining certain marks) with a second level outcome expected to follow from the first outcome (such as approval by parents).

This theory emphasizes the different levels of motivation that will exist in different people and managers should, if possible, have some idea of the motivation of their staff and, in addition, make some effort to enhance this by increasing their expectancy.

Things we hope for

There are many things people hope for in life, some of the key ones being:

➢ Good marks at school.
➢ To do well at sports.
➢ To get a good job.
➢ To make money.
➢ To own a house.
➢ To find love and marriage.
➢ To have children.
➢ To be healthy.
➢ To be content, if not happy, with life.
➢ To have a long life.

There are many less important things we hope for, of course, including that our favourable sporting team wins, that the weather will be nice, to have a nice outing at the weekend, to have a holiday before long, etcetera.

A major issue, of course, is how we deal with disappointment when are hopes are not realised.

When this happens we should consider whether the hope in question was realistic. If on further consideration we believe it was realistic/achievable, then we should:

➢ Extend the timeframe for achieving the goal.
➢ Consider alternative means of achieving it.
➢ Consider getting help to achieve it.

and examples of the sorts of decision making processes that might be employed are given in Chapter 14.

When things go wrong

There are many bad things that can happen in life, some of which can be most upsetting, for example:
- ➢ Getting bad marks at school.
- ➢ Failing and having to repeat a year at school.
- ➢ Losing a job.
- ➢ Marriage and family breakdown.
- ➢ Psychological problems.
- ➢ Physical health problems.
- ➢ Financial problems.
- ➢ Excessive use of, and addiction to alcohol or drugs.

When one has such problems one should always seek advice and help from family, friends, and professional to think difficult situations through and find solutions to them.

In the case of physical health problems, of course, one's GP should be the first port of call, whereas for problems at school teachers should be consulted. Family and friends may be able to help deal with minor psychological problems, but for major ones professional help should be sought.

For married couples with children, the 'breadwinner' losing his or her job can be a major catastrophe, of course, one that often leads to marriage and family break-up.

Whilst marriage counsellors often help with marital difficulties, finding a 'good' job can be very difficult, especially when one has been unemployed for a substantial period of time, in part because answering questions at interview such as: "What are you doing now?" honestly will greatly reduce one's prospects, especially if reference statements from previous employers are not highly supportive.

Indeed, in such situations, one really needs a credible advocate or supporter to accompany one to the interview for support and to help plead one's case.

31

Conclusions

In his 1994 book *The Psychology of Hope,* Charles Snyder postulates that hope has three key elements:
1. The ability to envision goals.
2. The understanding that there are alternative pathways to a goal.
3. Self-efficacy, that is, the capacity to muster up power and energy in pursuit of that goal.

Hope, of course, is very important in life, and perhaps there is no better example than the teacher expectancy effect because it gives a good example of how greater hopes and expectations can lead to better results and greater happiness.

Indeed, extensive research has repeatedly shown that more optimistic, more hopeful people tend to live longer, happier and more fruitful lives.

The first author recalls a pertinent remark made to him when talking to a lady in an employment bureau about being bullied into 'walking the plank' by a nasty new HOD several years earlier. She said: *You can't change the past.*

Unsympathetic as it sounded at the time, it is useful advice and, when one is pondering the misfortunes of one's past, as most people often do, it is usually best to limit the time spent grieving over past problems and move on to thinking more positively about the future, hoping to avoid or deal with any problems along the way more effectively.

Despite our best hopes things sometimes go wrong, of course, but even when a particular goal becomes seemingly unachievable, it is usually possible to find another way, perhaps also finding help along that way, to achieve that goal, and ways of doing this such as 'lateral thinking' are discussed in Chapter 14.

CHAPTER 5

THE WORKPLACE

A long pull, and a strong pull, and all pull together.
Charles Dickens.

Introduction

Most adults spend much of their lives in workplaces trying to earn a living. In most workplaces a hierarchy exists with various levels of management and the workers at the lowest levels of the hierarchy.

In these hierarchical organizations it is important for management to motivate the workforce in order to increase worker morale and thence productivity and profits.

The following chapter briefly discusses theories of motivation and behaviour modification, the effects of leadership communication and group loyalty on productivity, and avoiding workplace conflict.

Motivation

In management some understanding of the psychology of motivation is useful as it may help in learning to motivate the workforce.

Drive reduction theories

Drive reduction theories of motivation assume a hierarchy of human needs such as:
1. Physiological (hunger, thirst etc.).
2. Safety, stability and security.
3. Belonging ('love' etc.).
4. Self esteem.
5. Accomplishment.

Then motivation is based on the wish to reduce these needs, the level of motivation depending upon the position of them in the hierarchy.

Motivation-maintenance theory

Also called the Motivation-hygiene theory this recognizes two types of motivational factor:

a. *Motivators* (or intrinsic motivators). These include such factors as achievement, recognition, the work itself, responsibility and advancement.

b. *Maintenance* factors (extrinsic motivators). These include such factors as business policy, supervision, salary, interpersonal relations and work conditions.

The application of this theory is simply to realize that we should foster (a), which we can do at little or no cost, and do what we can to maximize (b), which we can do at relatively little cost.

Achievement motivation theory

This is that some people are basically more motivated than others and attempts have been made to measure such differences using such tests as the Thematic Apperception Test to assess to what degree a person is a risk taker and therefore ambitious.

This theory clearly does not replace the others but should be used to augment them. Note too that some studies have suggested that motivation is the main pointer to likely success in management.

Behaviour modification

With some understanding of the basic theories of motivation it is possible to apply them to motivate and hence modify the behaviour of personnel. This can be done using:

(a) *Positive reinforcement* - using praise, encouragement etc.

(b) *Negative reinforcement* - using criticism (which is removed when the cause of criticism is remedied).

(c) *Extinction* - ignoring errant behaviour such as showing off.

(d) *Punishment.*

34

Generally (a) and (b) are to be recommended but in time personnel will take positive reinforcement in particular for granted and ignore it. The remedy is to apply (a) and (b) alternately in some fixed ratio.

Other combinations are, or course, possible and, for example, (a) and (b) could be alternated in equal proportions with occasional doses of (c), leaving (d) to be used only in exceptional circumstances.

Morale and productivity

Surprisingly there is little mathematical correlation between morale levels and productivity and the coefficient of correlation between them is only 0.14.

Some idea why this is so might be found by comparing a company with a highly 'engineered' plant to one with a 'country club' atmosphere. Clearly we would expect productivity to be higher in the first.

We run into the difficulty of the question: *"To what extent are morale and motivation related?"* The moral, however, is that morale should be as high as possible (without going overboard) and that we should then focus on motivation using positive reinforcement and the like.

Applying motivational theory

To apply motivational theory we should set out to increase both intrinsic and extrinsic motivation:

a. To increase intrinsic motivation we should place emphasis on achievement involved in the job, attribute a measure of leadership to the doing of it, emphasize the prospects of career development and security, and attempt to improve the job design, including occasional job enrichment.

b. To increase extrinsic motivation we should emphasize the money and other rewards, emphasize the participatory nature of the work (in part by participating), allow as much team management as possible, and emphasize the need to compete with fellow workers and/or groups or companies.

c. In addition some priorities, for example safety, should be indicated in our efforts at motivation.

Frustration

We have discussed morale previously, noting that it may be related to motivation, or vice versa if relationship is taken to mean of the cause-effect type. Frustration may be caused by environmental factors beyond our control or personal limitations.

Frustration may also be caused by more subtle situations such as those involving conflicting goals. When there are two goals, for example, there are three possible situations:

1. Avoid - avoid, or two negative goals.

2. Approach - avoid, or one of the goals is desirable.

3. Approach - approach, if both of the goals are desirable.

Then if the negative goals (for example disliked tasks) are associated with a penalty for non-achievement each of the foregoing situations involves conflict.

In the motivation and management context, therefore, it is clear that in setting goals it cannot hurt to be aware of the potential goal conflict problems. These are not likely to be of the almost perfect dilemma type cited here, more likely some second goal will be a slight distraction, but at least the need for clear definition of goals with appropriate rewards is highlighted by considering cases (1) - (3).

Conclusion

The theories of motivation, behaviour modification, expectancy effect and goal frustration are both interesting and useful in management practice. Indeed knowledge of all these can be combined to potentially great effect.

Leadership and group performance

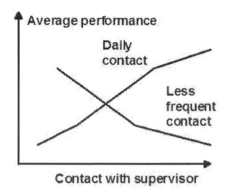

Figure 5.1. Communication with management.

Formal communication within a company will tend to follow the corporate structure. Effective communication can considerably improve productivity and morale.

Figure 5.1 shows the results of a study of the relationship between mean or average performance (or productivity) and amount of contact with the group supervisor. Clearly relatively frequent and regular management contact improves productivity as we would expect.

Figure 5.2 shows the type of result obtained in a correlation of worker performance and group loyalty, indicating that productivity improves if group loyalty is high. In part this improvement results from the (necessary) emergence of 'team leadership'.

The study of Figure 5.2 also found that correlation between the proportion of workers who took their complaints to the boss and group loyalty took the same ascending form shown in Figure 5.2.

In addition, the correlation between how easy the group found communication with the boss and group loyalty also took the same ascending form shown in Figure 5.2.

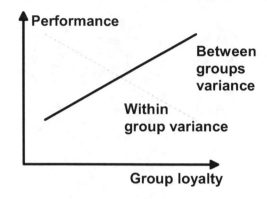

Figure 5.2. Performance and communication
with boss vs. group loyalty.

Effective communication (and hence loyalty) within the group and with the supervisor, therefore, both lead to improved productivity. In addition group loyalty improves communication with the supervisor, that is, the factors of group loyalty, amount of supervisor communication, quality of supervisor communication, and productivity are all interwoven in such a way as to suggest that if communication is optimized considerable improvements in productivity might result.

Figure 5.3 shows expected productivity compared to actual productivity for both the supervisor and the workers. Clearly the expectations of the supervisor are greater than those of the workers and are always fairly close to the target productivity.

The expectations of the workers, on the other hand, are for improvement when productivity is low and for slowing down when productivity is high, and are perhaps more realistic.

Figure 5.3. Expected vs. actual productivity

Unfortunately, however, there is no data from this study on the correlation between supervisor and worker expectations though this, of course, would depend on communications and, in any case, productivity variation is our main concern.

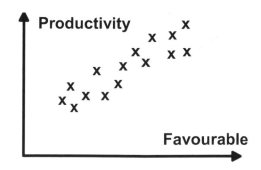

Figure 5.4. Productivity vs. supervisor attitude.

Figure 5.4 shows the results of a study of the effect of attitude of supervisor on productivity. There was a considerable spread in the results but there was sufficient correlation to support the finding that the more favourable the attitude of the supervisor (to both the workers and the job), the greater the productivity, as we might expect.

We might also expect that favourable supervisor attitude resulted in more favourable worker attitude and that the latter also results in greater productivity.

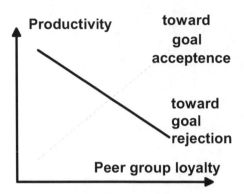

Figure 5.5. Loyalty towards company goals vs. productivity

Figure 5.5 shows the relationship of peer group loyalty to productivity when motivation is towards accepting versus rejecting company goals. Clearly peer group loyalty towards company goals results in greater productivity as we would expect. The results of Figure 5.5 are related to those of Figure 5.2, showing that group loyalty is a very important factor in productivity.

Conclusion

Besides those conclusions already made in the foregoing discussion, the following recommendations are suggested as worthwhile by the results of Figures 5.1 – 5.5:

[1] There should be effective communication of productivity goals.

[2] There should be thorough assessment of productivity results.

[3] Groups and tasks with low productivity should be identified.

[4] Group loyalty should be encouraged and groups should be motivated to accept new staff and 'loners' in a group.

[5] Leadership audits should be used.

[6] Supervisors should exhibit favourable attitude and communicate frequently and regularly with their staff.
[7] Group loyalty toward company goals should be sought.
[8] Supervisors should make themselves freely available to staff with complaints and other feedback, and make themselves easy to communicate with.

Generally, therefore, good leadership involving sufficient efficient communication of goals and team attitudes is likely to result in very considerable improvements in productivity.

It is also important, however, that measurements are made of productivity, group loyalty and management efficiency. The results will then be useful in identifying problems requiring correction and productivity results when favourable, for example, can be used as motivational information for supervisors and their groups.

Avoiding conflict

It is, of course, important to have a harmonious workplace free of conflict.

John Dean in his book *Blind Ambition* records that in the Nixon White House people used the term "stroking" to describe how they 'buttered up' people to get on good terms with them and persuade them to be cooperative and helpful.

In the same vein, Brent Cole in his 2011 book *How to Win Friends & Influence People in The Digital Age* includes the following chapters in parts of the book:
Part 1. Essentials of Management.
➢ Bury Your Boomerangs.
Part 2. Six Ways to Make a Lasting Impression.
➢ Smile, Listen Longer.
Part 3. How to Merit and Maintain Others' Trust.
➢ Avoid Arguments.
➢ Engage With Empathy.
➢ Appeal to Noble Motives.
➢ Throw Down a Challenge.

Part 4. How to Lead Without Resistance or Resentment.
> ➢ Begin on a Positive Note.
> ➢ Ask Questions Instead of Giving Direct Orders.
> ➢ Mitigate Fault.
> ➢ Magnify Improvement.

Chapter 11 discusses the Contact Hypothesis theory of human conflict, along with an attitudinal psychology model of human conflict, an understanding of these helping understand the causes of human conflict.

Conclusions

It is important, of course, for management to motivate the workforce in order to increase worker morale and thence productivity and profits. For this to be effective managers need to be communicative, friendly, and positive.

Successful businessman Thomas Joyce recalls General Eisenhower's autobiography saying: *Optimism and pessimism are infectious and they spread more rapidly from the head downward than in any other direction. Optimism has an extraordinary effect upon all with whom the commander comes in contact. With this clear realization I firmly determined that my mannerisms and speech in public would always reflect the cheerful certainty of victory – that any pessimism and discouragement I might feel would be reserved for my pillow* (Trump, 2004).

Lopez (2013) cites a survey in which 69 percent of people who felt their boss made them hopeful about the future were more committed to their jobs, whereas only 1 percent of those who said their leader did not make them enthusiastic about the future were committed to their work.

Group loyalty is also important, and wise selection of front line managers can help increase this.

Avoiding conflict, of course, is of the utmost importance and the preceding section gives a few simple ideas on this.

For "Mohr on management' see *The Scientific MBA* (Mohr, 2017).

CHAPTER 6

ADVERTISING & PROPAGANDA

*The broad mass of a nation . . . will more easily fall victim
to a big lie than a small one.* Adolph Hitler, *Mein Kampf* (1933).

*In wartime, truth is so precious that she should
always be attended by a bodyguard of lies.*
Winston Churchill, said to Stalin, *The Second World War* (1948-53).

The purpose of advertising

Nowadays there are massive media and advertising industries devoted to turning us into consumer zombies hoping that the products we buy will improve our lives.

The main objectives of ads, in approximate order of priority, are to:

1. Make the brand name familiar.
2. To give the brand a distinct image.
3. Attribute at least one key attribute to the brand.
4. Associate the product with certain usages.
5. To convince us that this brand is the best (for us).
6. To persuade us that we should buy the product.

To meet these objectives ads will involve slogans, demonstrations, comparisons, testimonials, and repetition.

Comparisons, of course, are usually of price, but sometimes also some sort of semi-official rating, for example safety ratings for cars.

By way of style, ad types include basic facts, 'mood', feel-good, social setting, slice-of-life, humour, fantasy, hard-sell, and anxiety/danger/risk.

An example of risk type ads are those for household insect sprays.

To make ads more appealing attractive female models, smooth talkers, or sports and movie stars are often used to promote products.

To give ads more authority statements by experts or organizations may be used to help persuade us.

To make purchase more imperative ads will scream of huge price reductions for a limited time, huge bargains for as little as two days only, and buy on the never-never deals with no interest for a year or two, if not longer.

In their efforts to get you in ads will go to ends which range from boring to extremely irritating, from dull and routine to the heights of excess and absurdity, from mere suggestion to downright pleading, and from slight desperation to screaming at us to buy the product.

More subtle are 'advertorials' of bought space in newspapers or conspicuous 'product placement' in movies.

For maximum tedium there are half-hour infomercials on afternoon or late night TV which sometimes repeat night after night, week after week, and year after year. In these and most other types of ads there are often trial offers, bonus products for quick purchase etcetera.

In monetary economic theory aggregate demand and aggregate supply are equated to obtain $MV = PQ$ where M is the amount of money in circulation, V is its velocity of circulation (in transactions per year), P is the price of goods in circulation, and Q is the quantity of goods in circulation per year.

Then if, for example, we increase Q we should advertise to ensure a corresponding increase in V or turnover.

One way of maintaining higher levels of production is through planned obsolescence of which there are three types (Packard, 1963):

[1] Quality: the product wears out in some planned manner.
[2] Function: a new product performs the function better.
[3] Desirability: the product is 'restyled', making the old version seem obsolete.

In the context of war [1] corresponds to a failed campaign, [2] to a new alternative plan, and [3] to restructuring of the forces to be used in the new plan. Then, of course, political leaders 'sell' the new plan to the public, whilst army leaders force it upon their troops.

Types of advertising

The main objectives of brand advertising and the various types of ads used to achieve them are summarized in the Table 6.1 (O'Guinn et al., 2006).

Table 6.1. Types of advertisement.

Objective	Type of advertisement
Promote brand recall	Repetition Slogans & jingles
Link a key attribute to the brand name	Unique selling proposition (USP)
Convince consumers to buy a product or service through high-engagement arguments	Reason-why ads Hard-sell ads Comparison ads Testimonials. Demonstration Advertorials. Infomercials
Instil brand preference	Feel-good ads Humour ads Sexual-appeal ads.
Scare consumer into action	Fear-appeal ads
Change behaviour by inducing anxiety	Anxiety ads Social anxiety ads
Suggest a feeling or mood when product used	Transformational ads (for long term usage)
Situate the brand socially	Slice-of-life ads Light-fantasy ads Product placement (movies etc.) Short Internet films
Define the brand image	Ads relying mainly on images, not words or argument

In addition, manufacturers and retailers periodically advertise bargains and "buy now!" special deals.

Targeting advertising

Maslow defined two kinds of needs (Lindzey at al., 1978):

(a) *Basic needs* such as hunger, thirst, sex and security.

(b) *Metaneeds* such as achievement, beauty, goodness, justice, order and unity, most of which are learned goals.

First, we must meet our basic or 'animal' needs.

Then we can turn our attention to the higher metaneeds which provide 'self-actualization' and meaning to life.

Both types of needs provide *primary goals* that may involve *secondary goals* such as money in order to achieve them.

Advertising usually targets the metaneeds of the *ego*. A Coke ad, for example, is not designed to remind you that you may be thirsty. If so, you might rush to the fridge and grab whatever drink you can find to satisfy that thirst. No, a Coke ad makes it look 'cool' to drink Coke with your friends and being 'cool' is a metaneed! So next day a young boy will want to be 'cool' when hanging out with his friends so they will all drink Coke and act foolishly, just like the actors in some Coke and Pepsi ads

Here again we see the downside of advertising, namely that increasingly ambitious executives will stop at nothing to sell their product, even if it has to brainwash the young into acquiring both bad behaviour and bad teeth.

In marketing to children, of course, familiar cuddly looking cartoon figures are often displayed on packaging and used to speak the lines of TV ads. Here, however, ads usually target the *Id,* the basic 'animal' personality that has basic needs like hunger.

Young children tend to eat in smaller doses and often so that almost any time they are awake is a good one to put a picture of confectionery in front of them.

One of the best examples of brainwashing, however, is the use of *consumer panels* of children in marketing research. The children are often asked what they will say and do to persuade parents to buy them the product.

Finally, the extent to which children are exposed to advertising is incredible:

- - "*it is estimated that children between two and 11 years old may see over 20,000 advertisements in a year,*" (O'Guinn et al., 2006).

Advertising, therefore, will persuade someone in your family, even if it doesn't persuade you!

In marketing to adults well known sporting identities are often used to market such things as golf clubs, household appliances and cars and houses. Indeed, this was the basis of Mark McCormack's very successful IMG (McCormack, 1986) and one of his earliest clients was Greg Norman who, marketed as 'The Shark', was made out to be a much better golfer than he was, and made an awful lot of money from TV ads.

When politicians seek to prepare us for yet another war they appeal to our *basic need* of security by instilling fear of the party against whom war is being considered, 'fear type ads' being a common form of advertising, a common example being ads for insect sprays.

Push and pull marketing

Some marketing campaigns use *push strategies* which concentrate on the availability of products. In this case the ads are 'basic' and concentrate on telling you the product name and where to get it. Examples of such ads on TV are

➢ A presenter reads a script while holding the product in question up in front of the camera.

➢ Ads with only text messages and a voice-over.

➢ Semi-humorous ads which sometimes use cartoon characters to present their message.

➢ Ads targeting children which involve cuddly characters and fantasy scenes and the like.

➢ Ads for junk food which play on having a high 'reward/effort' ratio (Govoni et al., 1988). That 50 million people a day eat McDonald's stuff is testament enough to the success of their advertising.

➢ Ads where the reader just about screams at you not to miss some bargain sale or to go to some cheap store.

Advertisements for 'basic' food, junk food, confectionery, clothing and home appliances are usually of the 'push' type.

Marketing campaigns often use *pull strategies* which promote the product in order to attract buyers. In this case the ads concentrate on 'image' to attract the audience to the product and the product name is secondary and *associated* with the imagery. Examples of this sort of ad on TV are:

➢ Sophisticated ads that show the product in 'classy' surroundings with actors dressed stylishly.
➢ "Laid back' ads were the presenter extols the virtue of the product with, for example, an island resort as a backdrop.
➢ Ads that use glamorous people such as movie stars as actors.

This type of advertising is usually used for higher priced or more 'up market' products, including fashion clothing, cosmetics, expensive furniture, luxury cars and overseas holidays.

One of the most important 'levers' in advertising, undoubtedly, is *keeping up with the Jones's*. This is exploited heavily in marketing cars and new gadgets of which the mobile phone is the supreme example at present.

Another powerful inducement is selling on the 'never-never', for example with no repayments for a year.

Ubiquitous advertising

Today advertising is literally everywhere. On TV in Australia there used to be regulations limiting the amount of advertisements per hour to something bearable. Now there seem like 20 minutes or more of ads per hour at times. Worse still, owing to the increasing cost of TV advertising time a truly bewildering string of ads appears in each ad break, sometimes up to about a dozen.

It is almost as bad on radio where there are sometimes as many as half a dozen ads at once on the higher rating commercial stations.

Junk mail from supermarkets and other retail chains has reached epidemic proportions. Other 'direct marketing' is done by phone and is increasingly irritating, often involving requests to complete lengthy market research surveys over the phone.

In addition, free local papers almost totally full of advertisements are also stuffed into millions of letterboxes in major cities.

Trams, trains and buses carry plenty of ads, as do train stations and tram and bus stops. Taxis and trucks all carry signage, as do many vehicles belonging to small businesses.

Shopping strips are becoming more and more cluttered with advertising signs above the shops, and sandwich boards and often products on the footpath.

Shopping malls are filled with advertising and more and more stalls with spruikers have appeared in them.

Sporting grounds carry more and more advertising and sporting teams now carry prominent advertising on their clothing.

Casual clothing often comes complete with the brand name writ large upon it.

The Internet is full of advertising, of course, some of it of a lurid nature.

Then there is the despicable practice of placing confectionery and soft drinks near the checkouts at supermarkets, resulting in many a tantrum as young children taken shopping throw a tantrum to get another dose of perhaps the first 'drug' of addiction, sugar.

Perhaps the most predatory advertiser of all, Coca Cola, has its vending machines just about everywhere, including pubs and clubs, office buildings, stations and heaven knows where else (they are probably there too!).

6. Advertising and Propaganda

Propaganda

Politicians, of course, use increasing amounts of advertising before elections, along with a good deal of propaganda to promote the political party they represent.

Wordweb 6 dictionary's entry for propaganda is:

1.   Information that is spread for the purpose of promoting some cause.

"The propaganda brainwashed many people."

As with priests coming from on high from a pulpit, politicians do likewise from prominent lecterns, all too often in history decrying some opponent in another country and ultimately urging the already brainwashed, beer drinking young men to go to war.

Using religion

In the West Christianity has been heavily exploited in marketing for example by
➢ The use of religious symbols such as stylized crosses in the jewellery business.
➢ The confectionery industry makes heavy use of Easter to sell chocolate. Bakeries join in by selling Easter buns and industries such as the entertainment and travel industries rely heavily on the Easter holiday period.
➢ Christmas, of course, is a bonanza for business and has become almost completely devoid of its original meaning. Indeed, the image of Santa is actually from a 19th century cartoon of a rich robber baron with some of *his* toys which he certainly isn't going to give away (Solomon, 1992).
➢ Not too distantly related to this are Mother's Day and Father's Day which are also exploited by, and were probably created by, big business.

Religion also makes increasing use of TV and radio programs for promotion and in the US some religious sects have also spent large sums of money to employ advertising companies to run PR campaigns to promote themselves.

6. ADVERTISING AND PROPAGANDA

New trends in marketing

Some of the many new trends of late include:
1. Healthy foods, for example low fat products.
2. Recycling.
3. Pollution free and environmentally friendly products.
4. Diets and weight watching.
5. Alternative therapies. Of these the list grows daily:
   a. Aromatherapy.
   b. Herbal remedies.
   c. Acupuncture and Chinese medicine.
   d. Group therapy.
   e. Exercise therapy, for example Yoga and Pilates.
   f. Transcendental meditation.
   g. Reflexology - and so on.

In many large cities where house prices have tended to become unaffordable to new entrants to the market there is a growing 'live for today' approach to consumer spending and this is seen in:
1. The growing fast food industry, including take-away food and packaged 'heat only' meals sold in grocery stores.
2. Increasing diversity in consumption of alcohol.
3. Increasing use of drugs which may perhaps be encouraged by the legalization of marijuana.
4. Increasing use of leisure industries such as gambling.
5. Increasing use of restaurants by young childless workers (who may remain childless).
6. Greater spending by young and independent working women on cosmetics, clothes, jewellery and other beauty and fashion products including hair dressing and magazines.
7. Greater spending on magazines, videos, books, computer games, music and other home entertainment products.
8. Greater spending on cars, holidays and other major items by young childless couples or unattached persons.

In these and many other areas there seems to be a growing market which advertisers are busy exploiting. In some communities, however, one or two of the foregoing examples may be on the wane.

51

Persuasion or brainwashing?

Advertising is now so effective in reducing us to consumer zombies that the results are comparable to those of classical conditioning of laboratory animals. In other words, it goes a little, if not a long way beyond just *persuasion.*

Colloquially, at least, most would agree that it would be fair to use the term *brainwashing* but, strictly speaking, this originated in connection with 'conversion' of American prisoners by the Communists during the Korean war in the early 1950s when The Three D's Method (debilitation, dread, dependency) was used in this context (Mohr, 2012a).

Sometimes referred to in psychology as *thought reform,* brainwashing is an extreme form of *social influence* aimed at changing a person's views without their consent and often against their will.

To this end brainwashing combines three approaches:

(a) The **coercive** or 'just do it' approach which is concerned only with *compliance* and not with your attitudes and beliefs.

(b) The **persuasion** or 'do it because it will make you feel good, happy, healthy or successful' approach.

(c) The group-based **education** or 'do it because it's right' approach which is much used for *propaganda* campaigns.

The 1999 Encyclopaedia Britannica describes brainwashing as **coercive persuasion**, noting its origins as a means of political indoctrination. It also notes that it is a *"colloquial term"* usually *"applied to any technique designed to manipulate human thought or action - -."*

The third edition of the American Heritage Dictionary of the English Language gives two definitions of brainwashing:

1. *Intensive, forcible indoctrination, usually political or religious, aimed at destroying a person's basic convictions and attitudes and replacing them with an alternative set of fixed beliefs.*

2. *The application of a concentrated means of persuasion, such as an advertising campaign or repeated suggestion, in order to develop a specific belief or motivation.*

6. Advertising and Propaganda

Indeed, most of us now associate brainwashing with persuasive advertising, political campaigns, mass media, and perhaps education, and media brainwashing is now widespread and a search for 'media brainwashing' on the Internet gives over 2 million results.

Just three examples of 'mass brainwashing' are:

[1] Claims that after WW1 psychological warfare research at the Tavistock Centre in London resulted in *"a theory of mass brainwashing, involving group experience, that could be used to alter the values of individuals, and through that induce, over time, changes in the axiomatic assumptions that govern society"* and that this work found application in both the UK and the US media (Wolfe, 1997).

US journalist Walter Lippmann was involved in Britain's WW1 'psywar' effort and was first to translate Sigmund Freud's work into English. In his 1922 book *Public Opinion* he wrote of the brainwashed masses:

". . . the mass of absolutely illiterate, of feeble minded grossly neurotic, undernourished and frustrated individuals is very considerable, much more considerable, there is reason to think, than we generally suppose. Thus a wide popular appeal is circulated among persons who are mentally children or barbarians, whose lives are a morass of entanglements, people whose vitality is exhausted, shut-in people, and people whose experience has comprehended no factor in the problem under discussion."

[2] Hitler had a well-oiled propaganda machine led by Joseph Goebbels, head of the Ministry of Public Enlightenment and Propaganda. Goebbels banned four Berlin newspapers in 1935.

[3] Claims that, because it supposedly misled the public over the 2001 WTC attacks, the American news media *"is the largest, most expensive, mass-brainwashing machine ever assembled in human history. It is a machine that so completely brainwashes the nearly 300 million Americans, that the Nazis' infamous Propaganda Minister Josef Goebbels would be envious"* (Wolfe, 2001).

Some of this is a bit 'over the top' but, if we consider that advertising has reduced most of us to brainwashed zombies wearing uncomfortable if not ridiculous jeans and carrying a mobile phone in one hand and a drink bottle or cigarette in the other, then 'brainwashing' is a serious issue.

And make no mistake, it must certainly be fair to call today's high pressure TV and radio advertising brainwashing. After all, in line with the original brainwashing of POWs, the victims are seated in a room and screamed at for hours each day with up to 10 ads blaring at them in each of all too frequent ad breaks (make that up to 50 ads per ad break in Brazil, according to Cateora (1996)).

After all, 50+ years ago advertising made about half the adult population take up smoking, a downright unpleasant practice in reality. If advertising can do that then it can make us do just about anything short of eating shit.

For this reason, therefore, the term *brainwashing* is used frequently in connection with the increasingly ubiquitous, repetitive and persuasive advertising used today. It applies equally well, if not more so, to the propaganda put out by governments to justify their every action, including those involving war.

Conclusion

The extent to which man has been persuaded, one way or another, to adopt countless religions, periodically fight wars over them, and in modern times become mindless consumer zombies is regrettable.

We should all hope that we will never be subjected to *coercive persuasion* or *brainwashing* in its 'original' form but few of us would disagree that we are perhaps now subjected en masse to something far more subtle, far more effective and sometimes, at least, far more sinister and detrimental to both ourselves and, in turn, the world we live in.

6. Advertising and Propaganda

Regardless of the politics of a country, however, politicians will always mislead the brainwashed public, and Edward Suchman gave useful definitions of some of the tactics used to cover-up failures in policy (Davis, 1974):

[1] *Eye-wash:* deliberately selecting for evaluation only those aspects that 'look good' on the surface.

[2] *White-wash:* avoid any objective evaluation.

[3] *Submarine:* 'torpedo' the program.

[4] *Posture:* use evaluation as a 'gesture' only.

[5] *Postponement:* delay needed action by pretending to seek the 'facts'.

An example of this, perhaps, in Volume 1 of the book series *Yes Prime Minister,* Chapter 7 is entitled 'The Smokescreen" (Lynn & Jay, 1986). The chapter begins with discussion of cuts in defence spending to allow for cuts in income tax, presumably because the latter help garner votes.

Seeing this as difficult, the alternative idea of increasing revenue with huge taxes on smoking is had, but eventually dropped, by this time the issue of cuts in defence spending seemingly forgotten by the absent minded Jim Hacker and, presumably, the public also.

One positive aspect of advertising and propaganda, perhaps, is that it tends to give us hope, albeit false hope more often than not, as noted in a 4/10/2017 article in the Herald-Sun newspaper by former Victorian Premier Jeff Kennett headlined: *In football and politics, hope keeps us going.*

In the present book, however, we suggest that one should concentrate more on realistic personal goals that might improve one's life, and perhaps those of others, rather than relatively trivial matters such as football etc. scores.

6. Advertising and Propaganda

CHAPTER 7

THE PSYCHOLOGY OF ATTITUDES

The body of science described in this book could only have been developed in democratic societies, where attitudinal influence is the form of control that is most often relied upon.
Alice H. Eagly and Shelly Chaiken,
The Psychology of Attitudes (1993).

The psychology of attitudes

Attitude can be defined as 'psychological *tendency* expressed by *evaluating* a particular entity with some degree of favour or disfavour.'

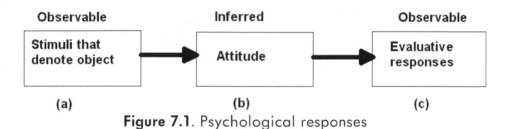

Figure 7.1. Psychological responses

Figure 7.1 illustrates the three types of response involved in attitudinal psychology. These are:

1. *Cognitive response.* This response is that of recognition of, for example, a name, a picture or other stimulus.

2. *Affective response.* This is a hypothetical construct and a latent variable. Here the sympathetic nervous system responds to (1) with feelings or emotions.

3. *Behavioural response.* This is the outward expression of (2) and may be a positive, neutral or negative response of some degree or intensity involving some observable action.

In this context conservatism, environmentalism or racism are objects. Then when we label a person a conservative, environmentalist or racist we infer an attitudinal position. Such attitudes are evidenced and also developed by the 'CAB' mechanism illustrated in Figure 7.1.

Schemas are cognitive structures that represent a person's past experience in a stimulus domain by a higher order or abstract cognitive structure. Then attitude is a subset of such a schema. Schemas have a selective effect on the remembering of information so that people have a better remembrance of stimuli that 'fit' their schemas and also for those that 'oppose.' This same selectivity applies to the 'output' of information as well as its input.

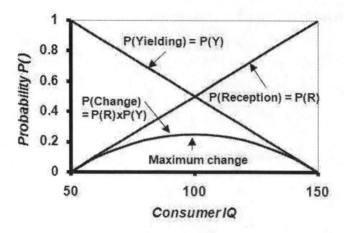

Figure 7.2.
Probability of reception, yielding and attitude change.

Figure 7.2 illustrates McGuire's reception-yielding model of attitude formation (Eagly & Chaiken, 1993). Here 'reception' refers to comprehending a 'message', for example an advertisement. This model postulates that the probability of attitude change is given by:

$$P(C) = P(R) \times P(Y)$$

so that a maximum change is obtained where the reception and yielding curves intersect, as shown in Figure 7.2.

One application of this idea is to 'get them young' so that advertising companies target the young and naive before they have the maturity or 'consumer intelligence' to develop resistance. Indeed, it is for this reason that the horizontal axis in Fig. 7.2 is labelled Consumer IQ.

Then, of course, ads need only persuade/brainwash some of the target audience and then imitative or 'social' learning ensures that many of the rest follow them.

Advertisements having achieved this, regular advertising reminds the audience of a product. Then in Figure 7.1 the 'C' response will be one of recognition of a brand, the 'A' response will be one of approval of it, and the 'B' response will be to make a mental note to buy it.

Learning curves

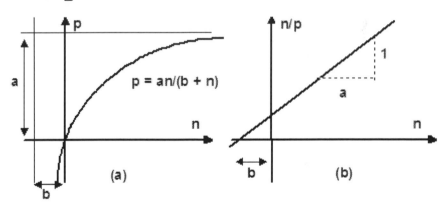

Figure 7.3. Mohr Plot for learning.

Suppose the degree to which a person or group has learnt something or been conditioned is given by the probability $p = 0$ to 1, and p depends on n, the number of repetitions of the learning process.

If we assume that the learning process is hyperbolic so that the degree of learning gradually increases towards 100% or the asymptote $p = a$ with $a = 1$, then this is represented by the hyperbola of Figure 7.3(a), the equation for which is $p = an/(b + n)$.

This equation can easily be rearranged to give

$n/p = (b + n)/a$

so that if we plot n/p against n the straight line of Figure 7.3(b) is obtained and the magnitude of the intercept with the n axis $= -b$ whilst, of more interest, the inverse slope of the line equals the horizontal asymptote a of the hyperbola.

In experimental situations this plot is useful in testing whether results are indeed hyperbolic and, if so, estimating the 'ceiling' value towards which some variable is converging. Applied to the memory of a single person we set $a =1$ and a typical result might be $b = 3$, $n = 3$, giving $p = 0.5$, or 50% memory retention after three repetitions. Here p is either:

(a) How well an item is learnt. People's names might be a good example of this. Ourselves, we often think one needs about three repetitions of such things to remember them.

(b) How much of a 'block' of information is learnt. An example might be a list of names where, because of *interference,* words at the beginning (the *primacy effect*) and end (the *recency effect*) are remembered best.

For a slower learner, on the other hand, b might double to 6 so we need $n = 6$ to get $p = 0.5$ or 50% learning.

Applied to conditioning of the populace by advertising, p is the proportion of the population affected and larger values of the asymptote b which flatten the curve might occur when there are two or more competing advertisers in the market.

In politics this highlights the advantage of dictatorship.

In education it perhaps highlights the importance of avoiding conflicting messages so that it is often best to learn one subject at a time.

Forgetting curves

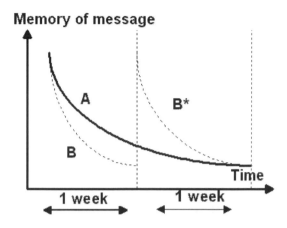

Figure 7.4. Forgetting curves.

The forgetting curves of Figure 7.4 also have important application in the psychology of attitudes. Here curves A and B are for two messages and curve B* is the result after the second message is repeated.

Then, when time has elapsed after an advertisement its 'residual' effect depends upon both the *primacy* (strength) of the ad compared to others, and its *recency.*

In Figure 7.4, after two weeks ad B* has greater recency than ad A, but less primacy so that they have nearly equal effect.

Such repetition of ads will ensure long-term potentiation of the remembered message, an important objective (Vander et al., 1994). Correlation between retention and persuasion, however, is by no means guaranteed and ads can be tailored to these two ends.

Expectancy-value models of attitude and belief formation

The most popular models of attitude formation towards an object, action, or event, are the expectancy-value models of attitude formation which are expressed as a summation of evaluations of each of several attributes of the object of the form:

Attitude, $A = \sum_{i=1}^{n} e_i v_i$ (7.1)

where e_i is the *expectancy* about the object for attribute i, that is its score on a simple scale as to the subjective probability or extent to which the object has this attribute, v_i is the *value* or 'evaluation' of the attribute on a similar scale, and n is the number of attributes considered (Eagly & Chaiken, 1993).

For example, a person is reasonably sure that a new soft drink Choke a Dope has nice taste and is trendy but considers that it is too expensive. Using scales of 0 to 10 for e_i and -10 to 10 for v_i he might thus rate the soft drink as follows:

Attribute 1 (taste): $e_1 = 5/10$, $v_1 = 7/10$

Attribute 2 (trendy): $e_2 = 6/10$, $v_2 = 5/10$

Attribute 3 (price): $e_3 = 10/10$, $v_3 = -5/10$

giving an attitude score

$A = (5 \times 7 + 6 \times 5 + 10 \times -5)/100 = 15/100 = 0.15$

whereas a 'moderately good' score in which 5/10 is given for each expectancy and value would yield $A = 0.75$, whilst a 'middling' score of zero for each rating v_i would, of course, yield $A = 0$.

In practice there might, of course, be many more attributes and, perhaps, we might average the score as $A = \sum_{i=1}^{n} e_i v_i /n$, giving 0.05 in the foregoing example, and such scores have been found to correlate well with attitudes assessed by evaluative semantic differential items (Eagly and Chaiken, 1993).

Information integration models of attitude formation

The information integration theory of attitude formation calculates the response to a series of stimuli i as

$$R = w_0 \, s_0 + {}_{i=1}\Sigma^n \, w_i \, s_i \qquad (7.2)$$

where w_i and s_i are respectively the weight and scale of a person's attitude to a set of n items of information, and w_0 and s_0 are the weight and scale value of the person's initial attitude (Eagly & Chaiken, 1993).

Here the scale value of information is its location on the evaluative dimension and the weight is its *importance* or psychological impact in relation to the individual's judgment.

Simple summation models such as that of Eqn 7.2 emphasize the importance of using multiple 'selling points' in advertising.

If the sum of the weights is required to be one then the model becomes an averaging model, but averaging models are more generally expressed as

$$R = (w_0 \, s_0 + {}_{i=1}\Sigma^n \, w_i \, s_i)/(w_0 + {}_{i=1}\Sigma^n \, w_i) \qquad (7.3)$$

The initial attitude parameters w_0 and s_0 may in some instances, that of religion being perhaps the best example, represent 'intergenerational' attitudes acquired from a very early age from family and society at large.

Such initial attitudes, of course, may involve *prejudice*, for example ethnocentricity or racism, and, as history shows, such prejudices are often firmly rooted and perhaps could only be modelled by assigning them an exceptionally large weight.

More important in the modern consumer society, however, is social or imitative learning and in this context w_0 and s_0 represent initial attitude acquired by social learning from a peer or social group.

For example, a person believes that Christianity provides good moral codes (attribute 1) and that Christ did exist and provide a good exemplar of how we should live (attribute 2), but doubts that God really exists (attribute 3). Even if God did exist, however, in view of man's disastrous history he has a low evaluation of this last attribute, so that, using scales 0 to 10 for both w_i and s_i, he might thus rate Christianity as follows:

Attribute 0 (initial attitude): $w_0 = 5$, $s_0 = 5/10$ (i.e. 'halfway' values)

Attribute 1 (morality): $w_1 = 8/10$, $s_1 = 8/10$

Attribute 2 (good life model): $w_2 = 8/10$, $s_2 = 8/10$

Attribute 3 (God): $w_3 = 2/10$, $s_3 = 1/10$

giving a response score

$R = [(5 \times 5 + 8 \times 8 + 8 \times 8 + 2 \times 1)/100]/[(5 + 8 + 8 + 2)/10]$

$= [155/100]/[25/10] = 1.55/2.3 = 0.674$

whereas a 'middling evaluation score' with 5/10 for both the weights and scale values for attributes 0-3 would give 1/2 = 0.5.

In contrast to simple summation models such as Eqn 7.2, averaging models emphasize the need to have a limited number of effective selling points in advertising.

Set size effect can be demonstrated by assuming all weights = 1 and an initial attitude score of 50 on a scale of 0 to 100. Then if all further pieces of information have a score of 100 the resulting weighted average score for k additional attributes is

$$R = (50 + 100k)/(1 + k) \tag{7.4}$$

giving the values 50, 75, 83.3, 87.5, . . . for 0, 1, 2, 3, . . . pieces of information, resulting in the hyperbola converging towards the asymptote $R = 100$ shown in Fig. 7.4.

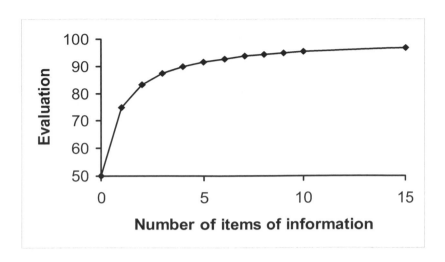

Figure 7.4. Theoretical set-size effect.

As might be expected, this hyperbolic result has the same general shape as a learning curve, emphasizing that there is a diminishing return for each additional piece of information about a given subject, albeit with the unrealistic assumption that every piece of information has the same weight (w_i).

The *three hit theory* of advertising, namely that three consecutive ads are needed to make people aware of a product, its relevance, and its benefits, would give (with $k = 3$) $R = 87.5$ (on a scale 0 to 100) in Equation 7.4, or $R = 75$ if there is no initial attitude, i.e. $s_0 = 0$ so that the number 50 in the numerator is omitted.

This is a reasonably good result and, indeed, the present authors often find that it takes three goes to remember items of information, presumably because they were not retained in the short term memory register long enough in the first instance.

Logical formation of attitudes

McGuire (1960) proposed that people maintain beliefs that are connected by the rules of formal logic. Whilst most of our early attitude formation is via parents, education, peer groups, advertising, etc., it is at least sometimes true that we take 'time out' to think about things and may reassess an attitude, trying to do so in a logical way.

As a simple example consider a confectionery product with the three attributes T = tastes OK, N = looks nice, and P = price is OK, and a positive attitude to the product is denoted as A.

Using a little symbolic logic in which $\rightarrow$ mean 'implies', $\wedge$ means 'and', $\sim$ means 'not', and denoting A = attitude to the product is OK, we can write $\sim P \rightarrow \sim A$
i.e. if the price is not OK then nor is attitude to it.

If $\vee$ means 'or' we might also write

$$(T \wedge P) \vee (N \wedge P) \rightarrow A$$

i.e. if taste and price are OK, or if the product looks nice and the price is OK, then attitude is OK.

The example is a little trivial, however, but no doubt we do indeed sometimes re-evaluate an attitude and use a little logic in doing so, but, generally, our attitudes are formed by the educational, imitative and information integration processes.

There is, however, scope for educators, religions, and advertisers to try and win us over with a little simple logic along the lines, for example, of: "You like to be comfortable so why not try - - -", an approach compatible with the cognitive consistency theory of attitude formation.

Mere exposure research

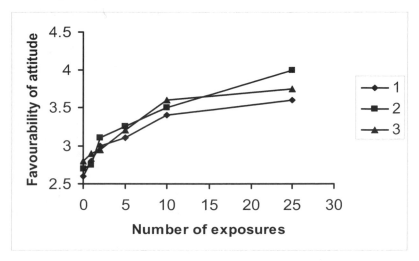

Figure 7.5. Increase in attitude favourability with increasing number of exposures to: 1. Turkish nonsense words. 2. Chinese-like characters. 3. Photographs.

Persuasion studies on message repetition usually focus on the effects of repeated exposure to *information* about attitude objects. In a classic monograph Zajonc dealt merely with the objects themselves.

Figure 7.5 illustrates the increase in attitude favourability with repeated exposure to three types of stimuli, showing a somewhat asymptotic behaviour similar to that of learning curves (Eagly & Chaiken, 1993).

This result is comparable to the size effect seen in Figure 7.4 insofar as increasing response is seen with increasing amounts of information, albeit repetition of the same information in the case of mere exposure.

It should be remembered, however, that oft repeated attempts at persuasion can also be irritating and result in negative attitudes, and some especially loud, haranguing radio and TV advertisements are good examples of this.

Implications of mere exposure in education are obvious, principally that students grow accustomed to new and perhaps difficult at first subjects, if not blasé about them, given time and repeated classroom exposure to them.

The latter observations might remind us that with repeated exposure we become accustomed to, if not hardened to, 'bad things' in life. For example, this is how children endure an excessive number of hours and years in classes and how adults endure jobs which may be, in reality, exceedingly tedious, arduous and boring.

It is also how, unfortunately, individuals become accustomed to essentially bad things such as cigarettes, alcohol, and drugs, perhaps in that order. This is, of course, good news for purveyors of such products.

Conclusion

Effective persuasion is all about changing attitude (where this, indeed, is necessary) so that some understanding of theories of attitude formation as cumulative or integrative processes is most important.

The results of mere exposure research compellingly indicate how attitudes to new stimuli tend to improve given repeated exposure to them, the bottom line being that it is by such means that we are reduced to 'consumer zombies' by ubiquitous modern advertising.

In the psychology of hope, the reception-yielding, expectancy-value, and information integration models of attitude formation are indicative of how more positive attitudes can be developed, whilst the results of mere exposure research show that, with sufficient effort, attitudes can in time be made more positive.

CHAPTER 8

MEASURING ATTITUDES

*If I can conceive it and believe it, I can achieve it.
It's not my aptitude but my attitude that will determine
my altitude - with a little intestinal fortitude!*
Jesse Louis Jackson, *Ebony,* August 1988.

Measurement of attitudes

One of the earliest methods of psychophysical scaling was Thurston's *method of equal-appearing intervals.* In this a panel of judges rates each of a set of attributes of an object (for example a new product) according to an ascending scale such as 0 - 10. Then the mean value of the ratings of all judges is the scale value of the attribute on the attitude dimension. For example, Table 8.1 shows the scale values that might be established for a new soft drink Choke a Dope.

Table 8.1.
Example scale values for new soft drink Choke a Dope.

Attribute	Value on scale 0 - 10
I don't like it.	0
It makes me feel ill.	1
It is very sweet and must have lots of sugar.	2
It has a nice colour.	3
The bottle looks nice	4
My friends like it.	5
it is trendy.	6
The price is good.	7
It tastes nice.	8

Then for surveys, the mean of the scale values of the attributes selected by respondents is their assessment of an object. To obtain more reliable results attributes that are rated inconsistently by the judging panel are not used for surveys.

Likert's *method of summated ratings* was designed to be much easier to use than the method of equal-appearing intervals but to be at least as reliable. In this approach a large pool of items which are chosen intuitively for their relevance to the attitude object is used (Likert, 1961).

These items usually consist of statements of belief but statements about behaviours or affective reactions can also be used. Typically each item is presented to respondents in a multiple-choice format such as:
1. Strongly disagree.
2. Disagree.
3. Undecided.
4. Agree.
5. Strongly agree.

Then, for example, a survey on attitudes towards women might contain questions like:

(a) Swearing is more objectionable from a woman.

(b) Intoxication in women is worse than in men.

With scores from 1 - 5 given to each of perhaps a dozen or so such questions the total score is then obtained for each respondent.

Desirably an initial pool of items should be pilot tested on a group of people to eliminate ambiguous and non-discriminating items which tend to result in neutral responses. This can be done by examining the *item-total score correlations*, each of which correlates the respondents' scores on an item with their scores summed over all the items. Then a good item will have a positive correlation and better items have higher correlations.

Likert Scaling is widely used in market research, for example to assess the response to political advertising campaigns.

Guttman scaling

This gives stimulus-person scaling simultaneously and results in a matrix of data called the *Guttman scalogram*.

For example, suppose we have five rods of from 5 to 7 feet in length (the exact lengths are not known) and ask each respondent to place a one in the Guttman scalogram matrix shown in Table 8.2 when they are taller than a particular rod. This raw data is then reorganized to obtain Table 8.3.

Table 8.2. Guttman scalogram.

	Stimuli (rods)				
Persons	C	E	B	D	A
2	1	1	1	1	0
4	0	1	0	1	0
3	1	1	0	1	0
6	0	0	0	0	0
5	0	1	0	0	0
1	1	1	1	1	1
* e.g. person 2 is taller than C, E, B, D but not A					

Table 8.3 is obtained by placing the column with least ones at the left, the column with the most ones at the right, and so on. Then the row with the maximum number of ones is placed at the top (this is for person '1' in our example and hence this is the tallest person), and that with the least ones is placed at the bottom.

Table 8.3. Reordered Guttman scalogram.

	Stimuli (rods)					
Persons	A	B	C	D	E	Score
1	1	1	1	1	1	5
2	0	1	1	1	1	4
3	0	0	1	1	1	3
4	0	0	0	1	1	2
5	0	0	0	0	1	1
6	0	0	0	0	0	0

The result is an upper diagonal matrix, as shown in Table 8.3, resulting in a score for each person shown on the right side in Table 8.3, this giving the ordinal ranking for each person.

The preceding example of Guttman scaling was for physical stimuli, when a perfect upper triangular matrix resulted. Generally, however, this is not the case when attitudinal stimuli are considered.

An example is Bogardus' social stimulus scale, illustrated in Table 8.4, in which respondents are asked to judge how closely they would relate to people of various nationalities or races.

Table 8.4. Bogardus' social stimulus scale.

	Acceptance level					
	Would marry	As a friend	Would give a job	Allow as citizen	OK as visitor	No contact
Armenians						
Bulgarians						
Canadians						
etc.						

Such attitudinal stimuli do not yield a perfect upper triangular matrix but it has been suggested that when about 90% of the non-zero entries do appear on or above the diagonal that this *coefficient of reproducibility* value is acceptable.

The Guttman scalogram has the advantage that the degree to which the reordered response matrix is 'triangularized' gives an immediate indication of the reliability of a survey. More complex to use, it is generally only usable for relatively small surveys, such as in-house surveys of consumer groups in advertising offices where it is an ideal tool.

Conclusion

Measurement of attitudes is, of course, especially important in many areas such as consumer and political campaign surveys. Though perhaps only applicable to relatively small surveys, the Guttman scalogram is useful because the degree of triangularization of the reordered response matrix gives an immediate indication of the accuracy of a survey.

Bogardus' social stimulus scale is used to measure the attitudes of respondents to people of different ethnicities, and is therefore useful in studies of the psychology of conflict, which is discussed in Chapter 11.

In the 'psychology of hope' simple Likert scaling can be used to quickly measure the degree of optimism of respondents to different life goals.

More complex Guttman scaling can also be used to give an accurate ordinal measure of how optimistic respondents are towards life goals.

8. Measuring Attitudes

CHAPTER 9

PSYCHOLOGY AND PSYCHIATRY

*Starting in the late 1950s and early '60s, the psychoanalysts set out
to convince the public that we were 'all' walking wounded,
normal neurotics, functioning psychotics ...
and that Freud's teachings contained the secrets
to eradicating inner strife and reaching our full potential.*
Jeffrey A. Lieberman, *Shrinks, The Untold Story of Psychiatry,*
Little, Brown & Co., NY (2015).

Psychiatry

Sigmund Freud (1865 - 1939) developed what he called
"the talking cure" or psychoanalysis which some regard as
the first method of examining the human mind. He also
proposed the division of the psyche into ego (our outer self),
super-ego (our conscience) and id (our inner self).

Modern psychiatry now assesses a wide range of mental
disorders, several of which are discussed in following
sections.

The field of psychiatry, however, has a disgraceful
history. As late as 1815 the Bethlehem madhouse in England
exhibited lunatics every Sunday and made a considerable
amount of money in the process (Youngson and Schott,
1996).[1]

At the Bicêtre hospital in France attendants used whips to
make the mad perform dances to provide traditional
entertainment. At the Charenton asylum the infamous
Marquis de Sade presided over theatrical performances by
the inmates.

---

[1]The word Bedlam is a corruption of "Bethlehem."

75

In the USSR dissidents were often confided to asylums for the insane, a policy no doubt practiced elsewhere.

The practice of lobotomy was particularly scandalous.

It can be traced back to Dr Gottlieb Burckhardt, the superintendent of a psychiatric hospital in Switzerland, who in 1890 drilled holes in the head of six severely agitated patients, thereby altering their behaviour.

Then in 1935 John Fulton at Yale University removed the frontal lobes from two chimpanzees, changing their behaviour greatly. Dr Walter Freeman, an American neurologist, was recovering from a nervous breakdown when in July 1935 he attended a seminar given by Fulton.

Egas Moniz, a celebrated Portuguese neurosurgeon also attended the seminar and two months later in Portugal he performed the first *leucotomy* by drilling a small hole in the skull and injecting alcohol into it to destroy the fibres in the frontal lobes of the patient.

The operation succeeded in making the patient less agitated and overtly paranoid but made her more apathetic and dull than Moniz had hoped. Nevertheless, further operations were performed and the procedure was refined by drilling six holes in the skull.

When he published he gave no hint of the downside of his procedure and Walter Freeman was bursting with enthusiasm to try it and he enlisted the aid of neurosurgeon James Watts to carry out his first leucotomy on 14 September 1936.

A week later the patient became incoherent and could not even recite the days of the week and when asked to write could only scribble nonsense. Her speech improved in following days and they operated on another five patients.

In November 1936 Freeman and Watts published a report in which they wrote: *In all our patients there was a ... common denominator of worry, apprehension, anxiety, insomnia and nervous tension, and in all of them these symptoms have been relieved to a greater or lesser extent.*

Freeman and Watts renamed the procedure *lobotomy* and made it more drastic by drilling only two holes in the side of the head and using a canula, the tubing from a six inch heavy-gauge hypodermic needle, to pave the way for a cutting tool to destroy targeted brain tissue.

Watts became so proficient that he could thread the canula through the brain from the small hole on one side of the head to that on the other. Though not qualified to do so, Freeman began to perform lobotomies on his own and became a celebrity in the process. He also simplified the procedure by using electroshock to subdue the patient and then plunging an ice pick into their head, usually producing a zombie-like person.

Often the procedure was repeated a second and third time and Freeman, a neurotic with severe depressive symptoms who needed 3 Nembutal to sleep at night, enthusiastically continued his crude procedure years after it had been discredited.

Such surgery had been performed on more than 40,000 people in the USA alone by 1955. Fortunately, lobotomy has fallen out of favour though it is probably still practiced occasionally.

The misinformation that allowed this brutal procedure to be performed for some 30 years, however, is all too typical of a world in which we are fed misinformation and brainwashed into accepting any new procedure or product no matter how dangerous.

Little better, however, is widely used electroconvulsive shock therapy (ECT) in which electrodes are placed on either side of the head and short bursts of high-frequency and high intensity electrical current passed through the brain. ECT can produce a strong amnesic effect, but it is not clear by what means this occurs (Atrens & Curthoys, 1982).

Psychopaths

This is the largest category of abnormal psychological types, involving the following behaviours such as (Davies, 1971):

[1] Assertiveness, aggression and bullying.
[2] Dishonesty and lying.
[3] Alcohol and drug addiction.
[4] Excessive sexual behaviours.

Psychopaths usually have two or more of the above traits, but are not normally classified as mentally ill, in part perhaps because they are so common.

Through their assertiveness, dishonesty etc. psychopaths often rise high in the hierarchies of business. Gillespie (2017), having had "many good managers" in his "various careers", cites a personal example of a psychopathic boss:

He was constantly meddling - - micromanaging the workplace - -. He trusted nobody and his impact on the workplace was devastating.

This boss made a habit of giving select people subtle but excruciating public punishment. - - The longer I knew him the more convinced I became that everything he said was a lie.

He cites a few examples of famous people from the past and present who might be described as psychopaths, including Caligula, Lance Armstrong, and Donald Trump, quoting Tony Schwartz, the co-author of Trump's autobiography, as telling the *"New Yorker* that if he were writing *The Art of the Deal* today, he'd call it 'The Sociopath'.

Mania

Typical manic behaviour involves a period in which an expansive, elevated, or irritable mood, along with enhanced activity and reactivity persists abnormally. During this episode symptoms such as increased talkativeness and grandiosity, distractibility, decreased need for sleep, inflated self-esteem, and excessive involvement in pleasurable yet risky activities may be present.

Such symptoms occur during normal mood changes, but it is their magnitude and frequent recurrence that may indicate a psychiatric problem. The frenetic and driven behaviour of mania results in a non-functional individual who cannot work effectively (Atrens & Curthoys, 1982).

The neurochemical alterations in mania are less clearly understood, but it is well established that drugs effective in the treatment of mania are those that antagonize dopamine and serotonin. The mechanism responsible for the therapeutic efficacy of lithium for the treatment of mania is not yet clear. Although mood disorders tend go have a familial background, the evidence for a genetic component is not convincing.

Depression

Depression is very common, and it is normal to feel depressed from time to time. Severe depression, however, is characterized by despondency, diminished interest in most or all activities, weight fluctuation not due to dieting, disruption in sleep patterns, psychomotor agitation or retardation, feelings of worthlessness, excessive quiet, and recurrent thoughts of death or suicide.

A professional diagnosis of depression is made, however, when a person suffers frequent and/or prolonged bouts of depression of more than usual severity, perhaps associated with thoughts of self-harm or suicide.

Major depression is associated with decreased brain levels of the neurotransmitters norepinephrine and serotonin, and the most effective therapy consists of drugs that inhibit the breakdown of these compounds.

Much less common, manic depression, or bipolar disorder, involves both manic 'highs' of greater energy and activity, alternating with bouts of depression or 'lows'. Manic depression is often treated with lithium salts.

Anxiety

It is normal to feel anxious about things ranging from minor issues such as getting behind with one's work or household chores, to worrying when a child is late coming home from a party. Many people have abnormal levels of anxiety, including phobias and fears, and tranquillizers such as Valium, which enhances the inhibitory actions of the neurotransmitter GABA, are used to relieve anxiety and relax muscles.

Obsessive Compulsive Disorder

Obsessive Compulsive Disorder (OCD) is a form of anxiety which makes people worry about certain things and 'overreact' to their concerns, the two most common behaviours being washing and checking, for example some people wearing away skin on their hands by frequently washing them, others repeatedly checking such things as whether the door is locked when they leave home.

One OCD sufferer, for example, feels compelled to do many things four times, another to count to seven between each mouthful of food (Carter, 2000).

Hypochondria

Hypochondria is an anxiety disorder in which people worry excessively about their health, for example just hearing someone mention a certain illness triggering fears that they might have that illness.

Tourette's syndrome

Tourette's syndrome is also an anxiety disorder, and certainly sufferers do appear anxious and disturbed when they have a bout of Tourette's and stressfully utter a nonsensical word while some part of their body, usually the face, has a 'tic' or twitches.

Asperger's syndrome

This is a psychiatric disorder usually noted during early school years and characterized by impaired social relations and by repetitive patterns of behaviour.

Autism

This an abnormal absorption with the self marked by communication disorders, short attention span, and inability to deal with other people.

In 2016 a Finish study of 258 people found that religious people could be compared with those with autism because they didn't view the world realistically, many believing in such supernatural phenomena as demons, gods and inanimate objects being alive in some way.

ADHD

Attention Deficit Hyperactivity Disorder (ADHD) is normally associated with school children who have difficulty sitting through classes without feeling distracted and wishing to be elsewhere doing something else. They thus have trouble concentrating and their learning is affected adversely.

There is much current controversy about this condition, many feeling that it is diagnosed too freely with children needlessly being put on long-term medication that may do more harm than good.

Dyslexia

This is an impaired ability to comprehend written words usually associated with a neurological disorder. The cause of dyslexia is believed to involve both genetic environmental factors and it often occurs in people with ADHD and is associated with similar difficulties with numbers. It may begin in adulthood as the result of a traumatic brain injury, stoke or dementia. The underlying mechanisms of dyslexia are problems within the brain's language processing.

Dyslexia is diagnosed through a series of tests of memory, spelling, vision, and reading skills and should not be confused with reading difficulties caused by hearing or vision problems, or insufficient teaching.

Treatment involves adjusting teaching methods to meet the person's needs which, while not curing the underlying problem, may decrease the symptoms. Treatments targeting vision are ineffective.

Dyslexia is the most common learning disability and occurs all around the world. It affects 3–7% of the population but up to 20% may have some degree of symptoms. While dyslexia is more often diagnosed in men, it has been suggested that it affects men and women equally.

Dyslexia should not be confused with 'mirror writing', for which Leonardo da Vinci was famous, some believing that he wrote in this fashion deliberately as a sort of coding.

Schizophrenia

Schizophrenia is a chronic neurological disease of distorted thoughts and perceptions which usually begins during adolescence or early adulthood (Sweeney, 2009) It has a strong genetic component, one which research shows may be largely physiological, and not a result of a "disturbed environment" Atrens & Curthoys (1982).

Schizoid people worry obsessively about being watched by others and being talked about, fearing that people know too much about them and have invaded their 'space'. When walking in the street, for example, they will worry that other people are watching them, in this way 'distorting' reality.

Schizophrenia is relatively common, occurring in about 1 percent of the general population worldwide. Because the incidence of schizophrenia among parents, children, and siblings of patients with the disease is increased to 15 percent, it is believed that heredity plays an important role in the genesis of the disease (Atrens & Curthoys, 1982). However, other studies suggest that non-genetic factors such as a "disturbed environment" are also influential.

In the last decade or two, for example, a correlation between excessive and prolonged marijuana use and the development of schizophrenia has been observed.

The biochemical basis of the disease may be an excess of the neurotransmitter substance dopamine, as high levels of dopamine and its metabolites, as well as increased dopamine receptors, are found in the brains of persons with schizophrenia. Further evidence for this hypothesis is that the drugs most effective in treating the disease are those that have a high capacity to block dopamine receptors.

Psychosis

Psychosis is any severe mental disorder in which contact with reality is lost or highly distorted, including severe schizophrenia. The drug chlorpromazine was developed and widely used to treat psychosis, by 1964 ten thousand peer-reviewed articles having been published on it. According to Lieberman (2015),

Like a bolt from the blue, here was a medication that could relieve the madness that disabled tens of millions of men and women - - the widespread adoption of chlorpromazine marked the beginning of the end for the asylums.

The commercial success of this drug encouraged pharmaceutical companies to search for new antipsychotic drugs, leading to the massive pharmaceutical industry of today.

Hysteria

This is a neurotic disorder characterized by violent emotional outbreaks and disturbances of sensory and motor functions. The term hysteria comes from the Greek word *hustericos* meaning 'of the womb' because ancient Greeks associated such highly emotional and neurotic behaviour with childless women. This indicates that man has long had an interest in trying to understand human psychology and behaviour.

Dementia

Dementia is simply mental deterioration usually associated with old age. Senile dementia of the Alzheimer type (SDAT) is a result of advanced Alzheimer's disease, a progressive form of pre-senile dementia that is similar to senile dementia except that it usually starts in the 40s or 50s, the first symptoms being impaired memory which is followed by impaired thought and speech, and finally complete helplessness.

Homosexuality

Homosexuality is on the increase. Once a trait one had to keep secret it is now rampantly displayed at gay Mardi Gras festivals, at gay bars in major cities, and in late night TV ads for homosexual dating services.

Some claim that homosexuality is inherited and a study of 113 people in 33 families in which at least two brothers were homosexual found a genetic marker on the X-chromosome (Xq28) that had a very high correlation with sexual orientation (Galton, 2001).

Genes may play a minor 'predispositionary' role but, largely, homosexuality is a learnt behaviour. Typically, for example, the normal heterosexual male has one or two homosexual experiences in adolescence (Robertson, 1981), and no doubt the same applies to women.

Those who become homosexuals, therefore, presumably do so as a result of imitative learning at an early age. There are, no doubt, also psychological factors involved, for example a lack of confidence in approaching the opposite sex coupled with the fact that there are earlier homosexual experiences to draw upon as an alternative behaviour model.

If alcoholism is to be regarded as a psychiatric illness, as it often is (Davies, 1971), then homosexuality is even more obviously a treatable psychiatric condition as well.

That said, most of our heterosexual behaviours are also learnt ones, many of them hardly natural or healthy, an example being 'tongue kissing', a truly revolting and very unhealthy practice like many other modern sexual practices.

Post-traumatic Stress Disorder (PTSD)

PTSD is caused by events of great stress and trauma in a person's life, perhaps the best-known example being that of Western Vietnam war veterans, whose vulnerability to symptoms of PTSD such as depression and suicidal thoughts was no doubt increased by feelings of isolation as a result of having fought in a war which many thought to be mistake in the first place, and which the West ultimately lost.

Losing one's job, or the death of a spouse or young child are also common causes of PTSD.

According to Cozolino (2002):

Someone suffering from PTSD is, in essence, in a continual loop of unconscious self-traumatization, coping and exhaustion. When these symptoms are experienced on a chronic basis, they can devastate every aspect of the victim's life, from physical well-being to the quality of relationships to the victim's experience of the world.

Madness, bullying and genius

A somewhat simplistic way of categorizing 'mad people' is to divide them into just three categories, in order of how commonly they occur these being:

1. Sad mad.
2. Bad mad.
3. Good mad.

The pathology of type 1 includes depression, anxiety, and OCD. That of type 2, the psychopaths, includes aggression, lying, bullying, cheating, 'backstabbing', fraud and other crimes.

A 2016 "anti-bullying conference" in Melbourne reported that "children as young as three are being identified as bullies amid concern many childcare centres and kindergartens aren't doing enough to stamp out the problem" (The Herald-Sun, 6/8/2016).

Recent research also shows that young bullies at school are likely to become anti-social adults, whilst a 2006 survey found bullying in the Victorian public sector to be "frequent", with almost 24% of staff saying they frequently thought of leaving the public sector. Similar findings have been made in Australian hospitals.

The third category refers to such people as 'mad scientists' whose discoveries are often of great benefit to mankind. Newton was no doubt an example, an accidental fire in 1692 in which he lost the records of 20 years of his work affecting him greatly (Egerton Eastwick, 1896), and perhaps contributed to him being remembered as somewhat eccentric:

> *He lived the life of a solitary, and like all men who are occupied with profound meditation, he acted strangely.*
> *Sometimes in getting out of bed, an idea would come to him, and he would sit on the edge of the bed,*
> *half dressed, for hours at a time.*
> Louis Figuier, *Vies de Savants* (tr. B.H. Clark, 1897).

Newton had two nervous breakdowns before retiring from Cambridge at age 42 to go into politics, saying: *Tis best to do a little well, and leave the rest to those that follow.*

No doubt these were a result of bullying, for example cartoons of him sitting under a tree and discovering his law of gravity with an apple falling on his head. In fact, this may also relate to him spending a period on his family farm, perhaps to recover from a breakdown.

Writers and artists, many of whom work in relative solitude, have also often been associated with depression, (Thomas & Hughes, 2006), Vincent van Gogh being a notable example (Sweeney, 2009).

Conclusion

Freud has often been accused of an obsession with sexual feelings (Gillespie, 2017), whilst both he and Jung seem to have been overly obsessed with the importance of dreams, leading many people to distrust formal "talk therapy". Chapter 12, therefore, discusses a range of treatments for psychological problems.

Chapter 10

The Psychology of Habits

How use doth breed a habit in a man. William Shakespeare,
The Two Gentlemen of Verona, act 5, sc. 4, 1.1.

*Television has spread the habit of instant reaction
and has stimulated the hope of instant results.*
Arthur Schlesinger Jr, In *Newsweek,* 6 July 1970.

*A habit cannot be tossed out the window,
it must be coaxed down the stairs one step at a time.*
Mark Twain, attributed.

Accommodation

Piaget used the term 'accommodation' to describe how
infants come to terms with their environment of a cot,
etcetera, and also become familiar with the small group of
faces that they regularly see often smiling at them so that, of
course, ere long the infant copies this behaviour and smiles
back. Thus WordWeb 6 dictionary defines accommodation
as: *In the theories of Jean Piaget: the modification of
internal representations in order to accommodate a changing
knowledge of reality.*

This early adaptation to a small group of 'familiar faces',
and the copying behaviour associated with it, is an early
form of social and imitative learning, a process by which we
develop many of the habits we adopt throughout our lives.

Then, of course, the many years most of us spend in the
all too long and drawn out education system inculcate many
other habits, whilst throughout our lives we are literally
bombarded with advertising and religious and political
propaganda, from which many lifelong habits are acquired.

Early learning

A great deal of what a child learns, of course, is taught by parents, other relatives, and teachers in a relatively formal didactic manner. Indeed, modern societies rely almost totally upon teaching at schools, colleges and Universities to train children and young adults for a vocation that in many cases will occupy them for most of their life.

Indeed, for many people learning becomes a habit, and they continue to learn throughout life by reading and studying subjects related to their jobs, or subjects that simply interest them, such interests often having been 'adopted' from parents and other life role models.

Imitative learning

Young children learn many behaviours by imitating or 'modelling' those of their parents, siblings, teachers and friends etcetera. Such imitation ranges from manner of speech to eating and recreational habits. Thus many children take up the same sports as their parents, whilst others may learn swear words and such bad habits as smoking from friends at school.

Social learning

Social learning is simply imitative learning that takes place in the larger context of society, rather than the confines of home or the classroom. It includes social groups such as friends, religious groups, and sporting and other clubs that a person might belong to.

It is by a combination of imitation of parents and social learning from a small group of friends that children may acquire an interest in beer and/or wine, for example, or worse still and far more dangerous to their health in the long run, illegal drug habits usually begin with social learning, for example at teen dances and parties etcetera.

Studies have also found that children with only one parent are more likely to smoke or drink by the age of 11.

Religion

Throughout history religion has played a major role in instructing adherents in how to behave according to guidelines established by each religion. An example of this, a Pope in the 1960s said something along the lines of: *Give me a child before the age of five and I will make him a Catholic for life.*

The current plague of Islamic conflict and terrorism that afflicts much of the world at present is, of course, in part a result of Islamic teachings based on the Koran's frequent advocacy of jihad against "unbelievers" in order to establish caliphates for a particular Muslim leader.

An example of the satanic Muslim religion, in one "barbaric" episode in Mosul 'Islamic State' captured a group of fleeing women and children and burned them alive.

Political propaganda

In like fashion to that of religion, political propaganda has played a major role in human history, usually with disastrous results as often clearly insane and greedy leaders seek power over more and more people and territory, often using religion as a pretext for their aims at greater self-glorification.

Hitler was perhaps one of the best examples, the Nazis doing an excellent job of 'brainwashing' the German people with a constant hail of propaganda to support them. The Nazis also provided their troops with massive amounts of amphetamines to 'energize' their military efforts, whilst Hitler became addicted to a cocktail of drugs including cocaine during WW2, perhaps contributing to increasing depression as the war turned bad for his forces, and ultimately contributing to his suicide.

Two factors in his hate of the Jews were

(a) The centuries old European prejudice against them because, when they had trouble being employed by Christians, they would go into such businesses as running pawn shops and banking, thereby getting rich.

(b) Rumour had it, and we tend to believe it, that he had contracted syphilis from a Jewish prostitute during WW1. Syphilis not being curable then, because antibiotics had not been discovered, the later stages of it no doubt added to his madness gradually as the years rolled by.

A globally widespread example of propaganda of sorts is the use of the terms 'right' and 'left' to compare capitalist sympathetic political parties and parties with more socialist policies, the term 'right', of course, being intended to sound 'right' in the sense of 'correct' or the 'right thing to do'. Here then is a major example of how the mass media in the West promulgates its bias towards the capitalist system that runs it.

The mass media and advertising

As discussed at modest length in Chapters 6 and 7, the mass media and advertising are the main means by which modern society is fed information, whether to 'sell' a particular religion or political party, or a household or other product.

The persuasiveness and effectiveness of advertising is, of course, sometimes remarkable, the Reception-Yielding Model of Figure 7.2 illustrating quite well why advertising is so successful in appealing to more 'gullible' consumers.

Indeed, modern advertising involving such subtleties as the somewhat subliminal effect of 'product placement' in movie scenes is often colloquially called 'brainwashing', and for that reason Chapter 6 puts the question: *Persuasion or Brainwashing?*

Recognition and *approval* are important factors in how 'consumer zombies' are brainwashed into lifelong habits of consumption, as emphasized by the 'CAB' model of Figure 7.1 in which cognitive, attitudinal and behavioural responses follow exposure to a stimulus such as that of an advertisement. Then, positive attitude or 'approval' is likely to lead to consumption of a product, and perhaps habitual consumption of it.

Indeed we are creatures of habit, much of our lives being spent in the company of just a few friends or family, consuming certain products we have come to like, and spending our spare time in certain adopted pursuits, for example going to the same pub or restaurant, and following a particular sporting team regularly.

Psychopathic behaviours

As noted in Chapter 9, this is the largest category of abnormal psychological types, the pathology of which may involve such traits as:

[1] Assertiveness, aggression and bullying.
[2] Dishonesty and lying.
[3] Alcohol and drug addiction.
[4] Excessive sexual behaviours.

Psychopaths usually have two or more of the above traits, but are not normally classified as mentally ill, in part perhaps because such behaviours are so common.

Bullying may be learnt by an eldest brother or sister, and the first author knew examples of both cases both within his own 'nuclear family', his extended (by his own marriage) family, and people with whom he was friendly for a while.

Evidently the eldest is able to boss younger siblings around from an early age, and often stays bossy with both these siblings, and perhaps others, if not most, people throughout most of the rest of their life until too old and feeble to be bossy anymore.

Bullying usually involves a 'superior' or boss, or somebody with psychopathic aggressive tendencies based on feelings of superiority, 'bad mouthing' the victim to their face with brief but hurtful and disturbing insults. These insults are repeated regularly to both the victim, often a 'loner' in an isolated situation, and to the bully's small group of friends and supporters who then repeat the same insults to the victim, increasing his or her feelings of isolation and helplessness.

In the schoolyard, for example, the bully is often bigger and stronger than the victim, who may be of the 'nerd' type. Indeed, the bully is often better at sport, but jealous of the victim getting better marks in class and perhaps occasional praise from teachers and others.

In the workplace the reasons for bullying by bosses or 'superiors' in the workplace hierarchy are often less clear, but often, for example, involve male bosses abusing women with 'sexual insults' that they are ugly, or that women in general are in some way inferior.

Addiction

Addiction to legal substances such as nicotine, a brain stimulant, or alcohol, a vasodilator and thus subtle tranquilizer, is, of course, very common.

Alcohol abuse can lead to problems in the workplace, home or social venues. Heavy drinkers suffer unusual brain shrinkage of both white and grey matter, reduction of the latter giving rise to the widespread belief that alcohol kills neurons (Sweeney, 2009).

Western governments have taken several measures to limit smoking, particularly limitation if not prohibition of advertising of cigarettes, in part to reduce the huge impact that the long-term health effects of smoking have upon public health system budgets.

Similarly, measures such as tougher drink-driving laws, earlier closing of some late night clubs and bars, and tougher penalties for family violence, have been put on place to limit some of the harmful consequences of drinking to excess.

Drugs, including alcohol and nicotine, have two problems:

(a) They don't really taste nice unless diluted enough by other things such as water and sugar in the case of booze.

(b) They alter the metabolic rate, resulting in changes in pulse rate and blood pressure, and contraction or dilation of blood vessels in the brain and elsewhere. Thus every sizable dose of most drugs gives you withdrawal symptoms, whether you realize it or not. If you have an overdose you will realize it and you might want some 'hair of the dog' (that bit you) as alcoholics call a dose of booze early in the day to help overcome a hangover.

As for quitting smoking and moderating booze consumption, the first author devoted a chapter to this subject in three books (Mohr, 2012b; Mohr, 2013; Mohr, 2015).

Increasingly, addiction to pharmaceutical drugs such as Valium prescribed for anxiety, or the raft of drugs prescribed for relatively newly 'invented' conditions such as ADHD and OCD, is commonplace and, indeed, something of a modern medical scandal comparable to that of the practice of lobotomy and leucotomy 50+ years ago.

The global illegal drug industry is now, unfortunately, along with the global arms industry, one of the world's largest. Some of the most widely used illegal drugs include:

[1] Cocaine and its derivates, including morphine, are highly addictive and have been widely used for more than a century. High quality cocaine, however, is very expensive, so that users often turn to crime to 'feed' their habit.

[2] Heroin, a narcotic that is considered a 'hard drug', is a highly addictive morphine derivative, intravenous injection providing the fastest and most intense 'rush'.

[3] LSD became quite popular in the 1960s but is rarely used now. It binds to serotonin receptors, only very small amounts having profound effects, including altered states of consciousness and hallucinations. In some cases LSD has been associated with psychosis, particularly when taken by a person with an existing mental disorder (Sweeney, 2009).

[5] Marijuana grew greatly in popularity from the 1970s, and is still widely in use, being easily able to be grown on country farms, and in suburban backyard and sheds.

Marijuana's active ingredient delta-9-tetrahydrocanniabinal (THC) inhibits release of the glutamate and GABA neurotransmitters, reducing cognitive function. Caffeine has the opposite effect of increasing neuronal release of glutamate and GABA, thereby slightly increasing cognition.

As noted in Chapter 9, marijuana use has been found to correlate with the incidence of schizophrenia.

[5] Methamphetamines, particularly crystal meth or 'ice', have become widely used in the last two decade, and are easily able to be manufactured with quite small and simple chemistry apparatuses in suburban houses and garages.

Gambling

Gambling is now a massive global industry, ranging from gambling on various sports to the growing casino industry. Gambling on horse racing has ruined the lives of many people, but it is gambling on poker machines which has ruined many more.

Many millions of people around the Western world are addicted to poker machines which might be likened to Skinner boxes in which rats quickly learn to press a lever to obtain a food reward, soon increasing their rate of lever pressing to hundreds of times per minute.

The video screens are part of the addiction no doubt, just as they prove to be in laboratory experiments with pigs and, of course, TV and PC screens have proved to be highly addictive with many humans.

Habits and hope

Many of the most common habits involve some degree of addiction, smoking, alcohol and gambling being some of the best examples. Most habits, however, such as the foods we like, the sports we play or follow, and the types of movies we like, are generally seen as relatively harmless.

A substantial proportion of the most common habits can be seen to involve hope, particularly gambling, when we hope to win, and in supporting a favourite sporting team, when we hope that it wins.

Regrettably, however, most habits are unproductive pastimes at best, often expensive, and all too often downright harmful.

For a better quality of life, therefore, we should seek to develop habits that are likely to have positive outcomes, for example a good work ethic which we could hope would ultimately be rewarded with better job satisfaction, better pay, and perhaps a better job and life.

Conclusions

Behaviours and habits are learnt from the outset by accommodation, modelling and imitative and social learning, as well, of course, by formal learning whether this be in the home or at school.

Such often lifelong habits as interests in and perhaps participation in music, reading, movies, and certain sports are acquired by both imitative and social learning, as well as teaching in many cases.

The mass media and advertising, of course, play a key role in modern society, informing us of current events, and also persuading us to adopt a particular religion, support a particular political party, or buy an advertised product.

Indeed, the extent to which we in today's consumer society are 'brainwashed' has all too many negative consequences and led the first author to coin the term *consumer zombie* (Mohr, 2012a; Mohr & Fear, 2016).

For a better quality of life, therefore, we should make a habit of focussing on productive and positive goals that, if achieved, will improve our lives.

Such goals might include, for example, a better job, making more money, and a better, happier, and healthier lifestyle as free as possible from bad habits.

CHAPTER 11

THE PSYCHOLOGY OF CONFLICT

There is no contradiction between saying (a) that contact tends to reduce the cultural differences among ethnic groups and (b) that contact also tends to stimulate efforts to preserve or increase these differences.
H. D. Forbes *Ethnic Conflict, Commerce, Culture, and the Contact Hypothesis* (1997).

Contact hypothesis

Forbes (1977) proposed that ethnocentricity of different ethnic groups tended to be increased by cultural differences and (presumed negative) contact between them, expressing the ethnocentrism within two groups *A* and *B* as

$$E_a = a_1 \, C_T \, D_T \tag{11.1a}$$

$$E_b = b_1 \, C_T \, D_T \tag{11.1b}$$

where a_1 and b_1 are assumed to be positive, and are measures of the latent tendency of each group to respond ethnocentrically to each other, C_T is the amount of contact between the two groups at time T and D_T is the magnitude of the cultural differences between the two groups at time T.

He further proposed that the amount of contact and the cultural differences between the groups depended upon their proximity, incentives for contact such as trade, and upon the ethnocentrism of the groups, expressing this as

$$C_{T+1} = C_T \, (1 + g)/(1 + a_2 E_a + b_2 E_b) \tag{11.2}$$

$$D_{T+1} = D_T \, (1 + a_3 E_a + b_3 E_b)/(1 + h C_T) \tag{11.3}$$

where g is a factor that represents the factors that determine growth or decline in contact other than the repulsive ethnocentrism and cultural differences of the two groups.

In equations 11.2 and 11.3 ethnocentricity decreases contact and increases cultural differences, as might be expected.

The denominator of the last equation ensures that cultural differences are reduced by contact so long as h is positive (the normal situation).

Contact theory has obvious application in marketing, PR and other activities involving persuasion, for example:

[1] It emphasizes that attitude changes with contact or, in general, information transfer.

If contact is 'positive', however, rather than negative as has generally been the case throughout man's sorry history, then equations 11.1 could be modified to reflect this by writing them in the form

$$E_{a,T+1} = E_{a,T} - a_1 \, C_T + a_4 \, D_T$$

where a_1 and a_4 are positive. Indeed, it might be hoped that the latter situation might be more likely in today's age of electronic communication and high speed travel. Moreover, it is in this situation that such equations might be applicable to advertising with $E =$ 'resistance.'

[2] It reminds us that ethnic or 'local' considerations are important in international marketing of a product.

[3] It reminds us of the importance of targeting advertising towards an appropriate demographic for a product, and that cultural differences exist between teenagers and their parents and, more so, their grandparents.

An attitudinal model of conflict

Mohr (2014a) proposed a simple 'first approximation' formula for assessing the potential for conflict between persons or groups. The basic formula takes the form:

$$A^* = A + xB + yC + zD \qquad (11.4)$$

where A^* = current 'overall' attitude,
A = initial or 'basic' attitude (based on 'known history'),
B = attitudes towards behaviours of the second party,
C = contact history between the two parties,
D = degree of difference between the parties considered,
and x, y, z are scaling factors that indicate the relative importance of the terms and here these will be assumed unity for simplicity.

Equation 11.4 can, of course, be used to assess the attitude of both parties involved in the assessment.

Here attitude is assessed in the same way as attitude is measured by the information integration model of Equation 7.2 but for simplicity only scale values (but not weights) will be given to a small set of items in measuring A.

Similarly, only scale values are used in assessing B, C and D. These extra terms add a great deal to the 'basic' A assessment to give a 'picture' of the 'overall' attitude.

Example application

As an example of application of the simple model of Equation 11.4 the attitude of a typical individual towards a hypothetical terrorist organization 'HTO' is considered.

To assess this only five items are assessed by simple questions for the initial attitude, behavioural, contact and difference terms in Equation 11.4. Assessment is similar to that used for the 'five-factor' model of personality (Larsen & Buss, 2002) and uses five possible scores:
+2 = strongly like/very similar etc.
+1 = like/similar etc.
0 = neutral
-1 = dislike/different etc.
-2 = strongly dislike/very different etc.

Table 11.1. Person's hypothetical attitude towards 'HTO'.

SCORE:	-2	-1	0	1	2
A, initial/basic attitude	Dislike/Like				
The people			0		
Their government(s)		-1			
How they look		-1			
What they say	-2				
What they do	-2				
B, group behaviour	Dislike/Like				
Sectarian conflict		-1			
Negative rhetoric		-1			
'Pushing' their religion	-2				
Threats	-2				
Terrorism	-2				
C, contact history	Uncomfortable/Comfortable				
See on TV			0		
See on street			0		
Close to		-1			
Talk to		-1			
Socialize	-2				
D, differences	Different/Similar				
Language		-1			
Economic				1	
Culture		-1			
Religion	-2				
History		-1			
TOTAL SCORE, A*:	-22				

Table 11.1 gives an example assessment for a hypothetical individual. Here total scores less than -30 are 'very negative', -10 to -20 'negative', -10 to +10 are moderate, +10 to +20 'positive', and more than +20 'very positive'.

Thus the results of Table 11.1 are mostly 'negative', the total of -22 indicating a considerable degree of disapproval. It is only very negative scores of less than -30 that might be a cause for concern if they were obtained for a significant percentage of a population.

Weighting factors can be assigned to items in Table 11.1 to reflect differing importance associated with them, for example the 9th and 10th items might have weights >1.

Effect of Societal views

The effect of the views of society on individuals and groups can be included in Eqn 11.4 by adding an extra term comparable to the inclusion of 'social norms' in Eqn 7.2:

$$A^{**} = A^* + fS = A + xB + yC + zD + fS$$

where f *is a scaling factor* here assumed = 1 for simplicity, and the factors x, y, z are also assumed =1 so that:

$$A^{**} = A + B + C + D + S \tag{11.5}$$

and S is the person or group's assessment of the attitude or 'position' of society, society here including the media, politicians, religious leaders, the public, friends and family.

Then measurement of S is done in the same way as for A, B, C and D in Table 11.1.

Table 11.2. Person's assessment of society's attitude.

SCORE:	-2	-1	0	1	2
S, perceived society view		Negative/Positive			
TV/radio/papers		-1			
Politicians			0		
Religious leaders		-1			
The public		-1			
Friends & family		-1			
TOTAL SCORE:			-4		

For the views of a typical person regarding society's attitude towards 'HTO' the result might be that shown in Table 11.2. Adding this result to that of Table 11.1 the aggregate score is -26, a 'negative' overall result.

A 'very negative' score would be less than -30, so the combined result of Tables 11.1 and 11.2 (i.e. -26) for an individual or a group is not of concern but worth taking some notice of.

Responses to conflict

When the group, attitudes towards which are sought, is in some form of dispute or conflict, whether this be economic, concerning mistreatment of a few people, or armed conflict on any scale, the attitudes concerning what measures should be taken against the group can also be measured in like fashion to Table 11.1.

Table 11.3. Attitudes towards measures against group.

SCORE:	0	1	2	3	4
	Level of support for action				
Government condemns					4
Cut diplomatic ties				3	
Trade embargo			2		
Public demonstrations				3	
UN sanctions		1			
War	0				-
TOTAL SCORE:	13				

Table 11.3 shows an example of such an assessment for a hypothetical individual concerning his or her views towards HTO's terrorism around the world. The total score is $R = 13$ out of a possible 24, perhaps a 'fail' mark by way of assessment of the group in question, but not an extremely bad score.

Total scores of close to 20, on the other hand, would indicate very strong feelings of which, perhaps, considerable notice should be taken should they be found to apply to a significant number of people.

The results of Tables 11.1 – 11.3 can be combined as:

$$A^{***} = A + B + C + D + S - (R - 12)$$

with the last term adjusted to allow for its different scale of measurement, giving A^{***} = -27 for the present example case.

Other factors affecting attitudes & conflict

[1] Hierarchical influences.

These include the influence of strongly hierarchical organizations that have very great influence on society and its individual people, some of these being:

(a) Governments of any type, whether they be monarchies or dictatorships have considerable influence on the populace by way of propaganda and enforceable laws, for example those of conscription.

(b) Political parties. Even when they are not in government, supporters of political parties are often considerably influenced by their views.

(c) Religions. These, of course, have had great influence throughout history but have less influence in the West now, whilst in contrast Muslim sects still have great influence on many of the world's 1.5 billion Muslims.

(d) TV, radio and print media also tend to come from 'on high' and also have considerable influence.

[2] Social norms.

Social norms have a great influence on the thinking of individuals and groups within any society, for example the wearing of scarves, veils and burkas by Muslim women is still very widely practiced.

The structure of society has also been an important factor. Fairly soon after the Agricultural Revolution and the formation of man's first permanent towns and farms the first small armies would have been formed to defend them, at first only temporarily.

Indeed, with the diversification of occupations that the Agricultural Revolution brought, permanent armies were one eventual result, notably in Rome and its empire, for example. Then, of course, given the availability of armies, there has always been a tendency to use them sooner or later, most obviously as the 'external police force' to deal with external problems, albeit a very large force all too often in history.

[3] Economic factors.

Economic considerations have often been the cause of human conflict, for example competition for resources, a good historical example being the Spanish Empire's enthusiastic search for gold in the Americas.

Man has always been inventing new tools and weapons, particularly since the Industrial Revolution. Now the arms industries have become massive and are able to considerably influence government policy in many countries whose economies have suffered a steep decline in their manufacturing industries in recent decades (Sampson, 1977; Thomas, 2006).

An example of the absurdity of it all, the CIA knew that chemical weapons were pouring into Iraq from Chile and South Africa in the 1980s. Cardoen industries in Santiago, for example, sent its chemical weapons, and the German-made artillery 'cups' or shells to contain them, to Iraq (Ben-Menashe, 1992). Then, the US later condemned Iraq for using these weapons on the Kurds and used this as an excuse for their first invasion of Iraq early in 1991.

[4] Growing populations.

Even as far back as early man's troglodyte days it is not hard to imagine an extended family group growing to the point at which a second cave was needed.

Similarly, when man had towns and then cities these too grew in size, needing ever more space and, more importantly, resources, particularly food.

This, coupled with man's habit of exploration, which no doubt dates back to his hunter-gatherer days and thence the hunt for food, has led man to engage in conflict with neighbouring populations.

Conflicts may have arisen simply out of the suspicion that the sight of strangers aroused when they suddenly appeared. Perhaps, for example, a spear might be thrown to scare them away. Then, of course, there might be retaliation and thus conflict.

As man's population continued to increase, of course, the tendency for migration and thence conflict must have increased, for example people leaving crowded and disease-ridden cities in Europe to colonize the 'New World' from the 16th to 19th centuries.

[5] Proximity.

Proximity also affects people's attitudes as does contact which, of course, is facilitated by proximity, the more 'negative' the contact the more negative the attitude formed.

Thus for tribal man, as with his chimpanzee relatives, proximity was a key factor in regular tribal conflicts.

Indeed, until only about two thousand years ago, human conflicts were only between neighbouring cities, regions, or countries. With the building of ships capable of sailing hundreds of miles, however, came the ability to explore more widely, and human conflict began to occur over greater distances and on a greater scale.

[6] Competitiveness.

In the Roman Empire, for example, there was a competitiveness in its governments, an obvious drive that made it wish to become 'bigger and grander' and go out and conquer other lands to achieve that end.

This obsession with competition runs all through the history and cultures of Homo sapiens, an example being our obsession with sport, or any kind of competition even if it is called a 'game.' It seems fundamentally related to the alpha-male behaviour of several other animal species.

Man, however, takes the alpha-male issue to absurd lengths, for example the original Olympic Games in Ancient Greece being conducted in the nude and, indeed, it seems to be returning slowly towards that situation now.

Equally, man has often indulged in war without good reason, usually because some loony leader and his acolytes want to 'beat' some other foe.

Conclusions

Very relevant to attitude also is the vexatious question of ethnic conflict and, indeed, the equations of Forbes' contact hypothesis do emphasize that, over time, attitudes change. Moreover, models like that of contact hypothesis could be applied to the effects of advertising.

The simple formula of Equation 11.4 combines the measurement techniques of attitudinal psychology with the concepts of the contact hypothesis to assess the attitudes of individuals and groups of people to other groups of people. The point of this exercise is that, when the attitude of one group to another is very negative, then conflict between the groups is, of course, more likely.

The attitudes of leaders are of particular importance, as it is these that may lead to conflict and war. The attitudes of leaders will, of course, be influenced by many of the same factors and stimuli that affect the public.

There are many other factors that affect modern human conflict. For example, particularly in modern times, alliances between nations have played a part in many wars, World War 1 and World War 2 being notable examples.

One difficulty is that, if two groups of 4 nations are allied, then a single nation attacking some part of another may quickly result in 8 nations being at war. In other words, the larger the parties involved, the bigger the conflict.

One fear for the future, therefore, is the increasing power of such huge nations as China and India, and also of the 1.5 billion Muslims around the world, so many of whom become involved in Islamic jihad all around the world, and to the extent that many believe that we have been in the midst of *World War 3* for some time (Mohr & Fear, 2016).

The numbers involved here are an order of magnitude greater than those involved in the two world wars of the last century and war between any of these three entities and another of perhaps similar size could well be the war to end all wars.

Mankind's disastrous history of conflict seems unlikely to end and we face other threats as a result of overpopulation, resource depletion, climate change etcetera. The authors HOPE we can solve some of these problems, however, and thus increase our chances of avoiding the extinction forecast for many animal species, including ourselves (Mohr, 2012c).

To improve our prospects we should push for *real democracy,* as outlined in Chapter 20 of *The Doomsday Calculation* (Mohr, 2012c), rather than the highly oligarchical and antiquated Westminster system that still governs much of the Western world today, and only then, perhaps, might there be any real chance of avoiding increasing global catastrophes and perhaps extinction.

11. THE PSYCHOLOGY OF CONFLICT

CHAPTER 12

TREATMENTS FOR PSYCHOLOGICAL PROBLEMS

Yet today's practitioners too easily forget their debt to Freud's original "talking cure" of listening to and analysing the content of a patient's mind, and his insight that a person can simply be sabotaged by the irrational within.
Tom Butler-Bowdon, *50 Psychology Classics* (2017).

Introduction

Chapter 9 discussed the early history of psychiatry, a wide variety of psychological ailments, and treatment for some of these was briefly discussed.

In the following section various broad classifications of psychological traits are discussed.

According to Gillespie (2017), everyone experiences some sort of behavioural disorder at some time in their lives, and low 'scores' or assessments of psychological traits are relatively normal. High scores, especially for prolonged periods, however, may indicate a need for treatment and several types of treatment for psychological problems are discussed in the remainder of this chapter.

Behavioural psychology

The ancient Greeks classified people as having four temperament types: sanguine, choleric, phlegmatic, and melancholy.

Hans Eysenck classified people according to three the 'supertraits' or dimensions of psychoticism, extraversion/ introversion, and neuroticism (Gillespie, 2017).

This came to be known as the PEN model, it's characteristics including:

Extraverts are is less 'internally' excitable than introverts so they seek contact with others for stimulation. They tend to be optimistic and lively, and are sometimes unreliable risk takers who care little about how they are perceived.

Introverts are more 'internally' excitable and moody and this 'internal preoccupation' is mentally taxing so that they minimize social interaction. They worry more about life and tend to be pessimistic, and have low self-esteem.

Neurotic people are anxious and stressed, they over-react to stimuli and tend to be emotionally unstable. Neurotic introverts are worriers susceptible to phobias and panic attacks, whereas neurotic extraverts tend to repress their fears and concerns.

Psychotic people tend to be reckless and mentally unstable, in the extreme being an antisocial psychotic or sociopath/psychopath.

According to Gillespie (2017), psychological behaviours these fall into three categories:

1. Schizophrenic:
   (a) Paranoid – irrational suspicion and mistrust.
   (b) Schizoid – detached from social relationships.
   (c) Schizotypal – extreme discomfort with social interaction.

2. Dramatic:
   (a) Antisocial – disregard for others, lack of empathy and manipulative behaviour.
   (b) Borderline – unstable self-image and relationships.
   (c) Histrionic – attention-seeking behaviour.
   (d) Narcissistic – needing admiration; lack of empathy.

3. Anxious:
   (a) Avoidant – feeling inadequate and very sensitive.
   (b) Dependent – needing care from others.
   (c) Obsessive-compulsive – perfectionism: rigid conformity to rule and procedures.

Treatment of psychiatric disorders

Psychiatrists and psychologists use interviewing techniques and tests to diagnose mental illnesses.

Treatments for psychological problems may include:

> Regular appointments for 'talk therapy'.
> Hypnosis in which patients are told to relax, clear their minds, close their eyes etcetera, eventually being coaxed into a hypnotic or semi-conscious state in which their minds are supposed to be open to suggestion, for example that they don't really need to smoke and should not want to when they awake.
> Prescription drugs, for example, lithium salts for manic depression, Valium for anxiety disorders, and several new drugs for ADHD.
> Cognitive Behavioural Therapy in which patients talk about their traumatic experience, sometimes in groups (CBT).
> Group therapy, for example monthly meetings of AA (Alcoholics Anonymous) or groups of people with OCD, the latter usually being chaired by a psychologist.
> Mindfulness meditation groups chaired by a practitioner in which quiet music is played and patients are told to clear their minds, relax, breathe slowly, close their eyes, and picture some beautiful scenery in their minds.
> Organizations such as Rainbows, "the world's largest grief support organization for children and young people" (Marta, 2004).

In extreme cases, of course, patients are confined to 'mental hospitals', usually for short periods in cases where patients are having bouts of severe depression accompanied with thoughts of suicide, for example, but for periods of several years or more in extreme cases of schizophrenia in which patients begin to lose all contact with reality and are unable to care for themselves.

In a few extreme cases ECT (Electroconvulsive shock therapy) is sometimes used. ECT was once regarded as causing significant permanent damage to the brain. Now, thanks to modern anaesthesia, it is much safer with a morality rate $1/10^{th}$ that of childbirth. ECT is used to treat extreme depression and schizophrenia (Lillienfeld et al., 2010).

Issues concerning psychiatric treatment

It was Freud who pioneered hypnosis as a means of psychotherapy, later discarding it in favour of "free association" in which a patient was encouraged to reveal repressed memories responsible for hysterical symptoms that Freud thought were always of a sexual nature, a view which many other psychiatrists felt incorrect, if not obsessive (Krapp, 2005).

A modern medical scandal is the way in which such drugs as Valium are prescribed for the long term to people. Such drugs are bound to be addictive and when patients forget to take their daily dose there will inevitably be withdrawal symptoms.

Such drugs, like the brain stimulant tobacco or the depressant and tranquilizer alcohol, alter pulse rate and blood pressure. Smoking two or three strong cigarettes in an hour, for example, will increase pulse rate significantly. The discomfort we feel when the next 'dose' of the drug is missed is known as 'withdrawal', in the case of alcohol overdose the symptoms being an increase in blood pressure and pulse rate.

Unless absolutely necessary, therefore, it seems madness to addict people to pharmaceutical drugs when they might only be briefly affected by some stressful event in their lives.

In an article entitled *Medication*, the *Weekend Australian* magazine of 10/9/2016 reported that: "Children are being over diagnosed as having ADHD – and now even 'daydreaming'." They are then put on drugs for the long-term and left feeling that they will suffer this really nonexistent disease for life, when in fact the problem will usually be one of poor study habits and motivation, often exacerbated by lack of a home environment that encourages good study habits, and the much too long and drawn out education system.

All this is good for the 'pysch. professions' as they can much increase the size of their practices with the many visits children will have to make for further prescriptions.

It is also good for the pharmaceutical industry which sometimes rewards doctors financially or with holidays and other perks to encourage them to prescribe their drugs.

New treatments

Examples of new treatments for psychological problems include:

> Many people with depression, for example, suffer from social isolation, and regular social 'chat groups run at local council centres are a simple low-cost alternative to psychotherapy. AA have long had good results with comparable groups for several decades, whilst groups mediated by a counsellor are also used for people with OCD.

> "Motivational Interviewing" in which patients are motivated to think positively etc. (Arkowitz et al., 2015).

> Just a few sessions with a psychologist in which the patient writes down their bad memory/experience and reads it out aloud 'as though it happened to someone else' can help reduce PTSD. Good results have been had in conjunction with the drug propanol (Miller, 2017), but no doubt good results could also be had using such 'thought transference' without this drug.
> Comparable to the latter, patients suffering many psychological problems can be helped by being told to 'couple' their negative feelings with positive ones.

Conclusion

It should also be noted that recent studies in which one group of depressed patients were given a healthy Mediterranean-style diet, and a second just regular 'consultations' with a counsellor, found that the healthier diet option significantly reduced levels of depression.

Notably, the 'Mediterranean diet' usually includes a couple of glasses of red wine daily for 'relaxational purposes', the procyanidins and other antioxidants in red wine being particularly helpful in reducing cardiovascular disease, and in this context it should be noted that brain function, and thence such ailments as Alzheimer's disease, are affected by poor diets that increase atherosclerosis. Thus 'natural therapies' involving healthy diet, including plenty of appropriate dietary vitamin and other supplements, and plenty of exercise, relaxation and sleep, improve both physical and mental health (Mohr, 2012b, 2013, 2015).

The authors therefore recommend improved diet and lifestyle, including occasional contact with supportive and helpful friends and neighbours, as a means of improving mental health, perhaps in conjunction with professional counselling if need be, though in most cases the latter should only be required for the short term, for example to help deal with a particular event such as a death in the family, divorce etcetera.

In the case of marriage problems, of course, marriage guidance counsellors have traditionally been used by many people, whilst some Christian church groups now run more general counselling services in offices run at sites not connected/adjacent to a church.

In choosing a counsellor one might, for example, be wary of those overly obsessed with sexual issues or dreams as being the root of many problems, as the authors believe Sigmund Freud and Carl Jung were.

When professional 'talk therapy' is used, however, the patient should take care to choose a counsellor intelligent enough to quickly work out what memories etc. are affecting them and suggest sensible and effective ideas to deal with any 'mental problems', and using pharmaceutical drugs only when clearly necessary, and then only for the short or medium term.

In dealing with psychological problems in children, of course, teachers should also be involved as soon as possible to help children cope. As with adults, involving children with sports or other activity or 'interest' groups can provide social connections that may reduce such issues as depression, and autism, and ADHD.

Finally, not that, in emergency situations people in psychological crisis should establish phone contact with organizations such as Lifeline and Beyond Blue.

CHAPTER 13

BUILDING SELF-CONFIDENCE AND HOPE

*Faith is a charisma not granted to all; instead man has the gift
of thought, which can strive after the highest things.*
Carl Jung, *A Psychological Approach to the Dogma of the Trinity,*
(1958), *Collected Works,* vol. 2 (1969).

Self-esteem and self-confidence

Some psychologists argue that self-esteem has two components: *self-efficacy* and *self-respect* (Krapp, 2005), and in order to increase self-belief often counsel patients to:

(a) Repeat to themselves such statements of affirmation as: *"I believe in myself"* to increase self-belief.

(b) Associate with positive people to obtain encouragement and support.

(c) List their past successes and review this list periodically to increase their levels of optimism.

Dr Robert Anthony in his 2010 book *The Ultimate Secrets of Total Self-Confidence* describes a "simple but very effective learning technique" in which over a period of only 21 days patients "break an old destructive habit and form a new positive one."

Various chapters encourage readers to:
- ➤ "Dehypnotise" themselves.
- ➤ Develop self-reliance.
- ➤ Think positively.
- ➤ Use "creative imagination".
- ➤ Develop a "direct action worksheet".
- ➤ "Get the smile habit".

117

The final chapter concludes that a positive mental attitude gives a person self-confidence.

It could also be added, of course, that a positive attitude givens one hope, and with hope comes some degree of confidence.

Self-regulation

Bandura's social-cognitive theory holds that people are capable of self-regulation and thus controlling their own behaviour, and that the self-regulation process has three parts (Krapp, 2005):

[1] Self-observation: tracking one's own thoughts, feelings and behaviours.

[2] Judgement: comparing oneself to standards set by oneself or, preferably, others.

[3] Self-response: rewarding oneself for doing well and punishing oneself for doing badly.

For example, a student doing poorly at mathematics can self-regulate their performance by (Krapp, 2005):

[1] Write down their negative thoughts associated with maths classes, homework, and tests.

[2] Set a realistic goal for improvement, for example if the student is getting C grades, they should be somewhat optimistic and aim for B grades, not C+ as this is not a sufficiently rewarding goal, and not A+ as this is not a realistic goal.

[3] Note but not dwell too much on any lack of improvement, but celebrate improvement when it comes.

Self-assessment

Sensible and accurate self-assessment is, of course, very important throughout life, and this should include several of the key facets of one's life, and Table 13.1 is an example 'life-assessment' for a married person in their mid-30s with a job and two children.

Table 13.1. Self-assessment for married person.

Factor	Present situation	Score/10
Job	OK	6
Marriage	OK	7
Family finances	?	5
Home life	Good	8
Child 1	Problems	4
Child 2	Good	8
House	OK	7
Car	Old	6
Social life	Very little	3
Total score/100		**54**

The total score is mediocre, to say the least, and perhaps a better job could be hoped for to improve it, and thence the family finances and situation in general.

If weights were added to each factor, as in the Expectancy-Value and Information Integration models of attitude formation discussed in Chapter 7, then a better assessment is obtained. A relatively high weight would be given to the 'job' factor, of course, as this affects most, if not all, of the other 9 factors.

In the case of a school-age child, of course, the factors would by very different, including marks at school, friends, extra-curricular activities such as sports, 'pocket money', and perhaps food as children, of course, have to do as they are told on most things, including what they eat, and their earliest signs of discontent are often diet-related.

Social support

When things go wrong it is, of course, helpful to have supportive people, whether they be relatives, friends, or counsellors, to turn to for advice and moral support.

Such people can provide help and encouragement that may provide hope in the most difficult of circumstances, and hope alone in most cases will help one cope in the short term.

Then, in the longer term, one can begin to fix the problem(s) in question, or 'move on' from them to work towards new goals.

Successful businesswoman Lillian Vernon recalls: *My father told me I had talent and a good idea for starting a business and I should never let anything get in the way of fulfilling my dream, or I would regret it for the rest of my life,* concluding: *So don't let challenges, setbacks, or detractors defeat or discourage you. If you believe in yourself and think positively, you will succeed* (Trump, 2004).

Conclusions

For best results one must, of course, tackle life and its occasional problems with the inter-related personal characteristics and behaviours:

- ➢ Self-esteem.
- ➢ Self-confidence.
- ➢ Self-reliance.
- ➢ Self-belief.
- ➢ Self-regulation or control.
- ➢ Self-assessment in similar fashion to the Expectation-Value and Information Integration models of attitude formation and assessment.
- ➢ Realistic goal-setting.
- ➢ Support from friends etc. with problems, and in achieving one's goals.

Then, if one has self-confidence, achievable goals etc., one also has HOPE without which, of course, life can be unbearable.

The following chapter discusses the important topics of creative thinking, problem solving, and decision making, outlining several techniques for planning a successful life.

CHAPTER 14

PLANNING FOR SUCCESS

*Planning is as natural to the process of success
as its absence is to the process of failure.*
Robin Seiger, *Natural Born Winners* (1999).

Introduction

All too many of us go through life without sufficient
planning, in part because we grow up with our lives largely
controlled by parents and educators. Even at a young age,
however, we should acquire the habit of planning our lives,
at least in part, for example planning weekend activities with
friends, and joining in planning of family activities.

In adult life, of course, planning is very important, for
example planning personal and family activities and
finances. We should also plan our working lives as far as
possible, including in such plans our goals and aspirations,
for example for better pay or a better job.

The following chapter gives examples of some of the
common tools that can be used for planning, beginning with
creative thinking to come up with ideas and goals for which
we can then make plans.

Creative thinking

Divergent thinking involves considering a number of
alternatives, some of which may be new and/or impractical,
rather than seeking a single logical solution.

Creative thinking involves finding novel but practical
solutions to a problem or task using divergent thinking and
may occur in three stages (Morgan et al., 1979):

[1] Preparation: define the facts and materials needed for the new solution.

[2] Incubation: acquire further information, think about, and 'sleep on' the problem.

{3] Assembly: combine information to find the solution.

Creativity may be enhanced by 'undirected' or *autistic thinking*, as occurs in dreams, in which one's own 'personal' and unique concepts are freely associated. This is accomplished by *brainstorming* in which the mind is allowed to roam freely through as many ideas as possible.

Creative people enjoy creating things, are assertive, have a risk taking approach, tend to be impulsive, dislike constraints, like a little complexity, are objective about their efforts (i.e., able to critically examine them), and accept feedback from others.

Among other characteristics, creative people may also be intuitive, perceptive, ingenious, industrious, persistent, independent, unconventional, courageous, uninhibited, moody, self-centred and eccentric.

In conclusion: *"- - creativity is central to a rich, meaningful life"* (Butler-Bowdon, 2017). More important, it is a key component of *real IQ* (Mohr, Sinclair & Fear, 2017).

Sometimes *brainstorming* helps solve a problem, and group brainstorming has been found effective because:

[1] People tend to have twice as many ideas in the group situation because of the more stimulating environment, 'cross fertilization' of ideas and arousal of competitive spirit.

[2] Alternation of individual and group thinking improves results.

[3] As more ideas are produced they tend to improve.

[4] Second sessions a few days later improve results because of the 'incubation' process so important in creative thinking.

[5] The group uses *critical thinking* to evaluate the ideas.

Problem solving

Problems can be attacked in three stages:

[1] Defining the problem
At first this might involve realizing that a problem exists. Then we need to determine:

(a) What is the initial situation, i.e., what is known about the problem?

(b) What is the goal?

(c) What are the restrictions or *constraints*?

(d) What moves or *operations* are required to reach the goal?

[2] Generating possible solutions
Solutions to a problem can be obtained by such *strategies* as:

(a) In the case of mathematics problems, for example, *algorithms* can be used to try large numbers of solutions on a computer.

(b) Use an existing *heuristic rule* or 'rule of thumb.'

(c) Redefine the problem, for example by breaking it down into stages and seeking a 'solution' for each stage. Such *means-end analysis* is sometimes more successful if the problem is examined by working backwards through these stages.

(d) Use a new arrangement of existing techniques or materials.

(e) Invent new techniques or materials, i.e., use *insight learning*. This requires *creative thinking* which, as described earlier, often involves *incubation* periods.

Creative thinking can be inhibited by:

(i) *Functional fixedness,* the difficulty of imagining new uses for materials or devices.

(ii) *Mental set,* the difficulty in finding new strategies for approaching a problem. Mental set can be induced by recent experiences or old habits.

[3] Testing and evaluating the solutions

Alternative solutions are tested to see how well they work in relation to predetermined criteria.

Sometimes problems can be solved by *trial and error* so that trial solutions are repetitively adjusted until satisfactory.

Selection of the best solution from a number of alternatives should be done with a quantitative basis.

Lateral thinking

Edward de Bono proposed lateral thinking as an alternative to logical or *vertical* thinking. Some of the features of lateral thinking are:

➢ Steps can be jumped (and 'filled' later).

➢ Steps need not be 'correct' so long as the conclusion is correct and may be made in order to *generate* a new direction or branch.

➢ Interpretation of task criteria and alternative solution properties can be changed and the process is not *finite,* that is it need not reach a conclusion in any given time.

➢ It is *probabilistic* so that less obvious solutions are considered so that the best solution is obtained (if a valid solution exists).

De Bono (1982) recommends use of the word PO:

"PO is the laxative of language"

as an alternative to the words 'yes' and 'no' to emphasize that lateral thinking is not quick to say no to less obvious solutions and, rather than stop at obstacles to a solution, one should *go around* them by such means as those summarized above.

Whilst 'po' seems a somewhat trivial, if not absurd, idea, it may have some merit for many of us do indeed have a tendency to persist trying to solve some problems rather than 'go around' them.

Selecting the best candidate for a job is a good example. If this is done with lateral thinking:

[1] Some criteria might be ignored or downgraded in importance so that more candidates will be considered.

[2] Those that do not satisfy some criteria might remain under consideration.

[3] Candidates not at the top of the list are re-evaluated.

Lateral thinking is better understood with reference to the decision trees described in a later section. In these lateral thinking might encourage us to consider branches that have lower probabilities of success.

The bottom line, however, is that lateral thinking simply involves considering more than one possible solution to a problem or task.

In this context the first author uses the term 'bilemma' when one has difficulty deciding between two alternatives, and then the term 'trilemma' when there are three alternatives, viewing the latter as the preferred situation as he feels it fairly easy to knock out one of three alternatives.

As in 'Mohr's Law of Politics', deciding between two almost equal alternatives is harder. In the farcical and outdated Westminster system, for example, the 2 main parties are relatively similar in policies, incompetence etcetera, so many a voter makes up their mind on which side of the political fence to place their vote only at the last minute.

Mohr's laws of decisions

Essentially, the major problem of the human race is the habit of making bad decisions.

Some of us, at least, are very good at creative thinking to produce new ideas and products, and others are good at making the things we most need such as food, clothing and shelter.

As a result of the devastatingly accurate Peter Principle, all too many of our leaders and managers are, more often than not, guilty of bad decisions, if not corruption.

If a leader commits us to an unjustified war then, just as architects do, he praises his mistake. If a worker makes a small error or two he is dismissed.

Self-evident as they may be, Mohr's Laws of Decision (Mohr, 2014b) are some help:

1) Don't rush.

2) Don't take the first offer or run with the first idea.

3) Look for alternative ideas and build an ideas/options list.

4) List the requirements or inputs for each option.

5) List the results or outputs for each option.

6) Calculate the ratio of the outputs to inputs for each option.

7) Double check the accuracy of 4 - 6.

8) Select the option with the highest output/input ratio.

9) Ask at least a second opinion.

10) Sleep on it.

The analysis of steps 4 - 6 corresponds to *cost-benefit* analysis, a simple technique widely used in economic studies of infrastructure and other plans to decide on the best program of work.

Many a housewife probably uses a somewhat similar decision making approach but the usually moronic politicians who run countries find such stuff hard going and have to employ thousands of economists and statisticians to perform these rudimentary analyses.

Needless to say they usually get it wrong, often when somebody's palm is greased, for example by a construction company seeking the contract for a major government project.

Decision tables

A good example is the following table of the performance of three categories of stocks and shares under boom, steady and slump market conditions.

	Boom (a)	Steady (b)	Slump (c)
Gilt edged (x)	5 %	5	5
Speculative (y)	20	0	-10
Unit trusts (z)	10	5	0

What then is the best mix of shares to buy?

The *deterministic solution* is as follows. For a 10 year cycle time in business conditions assume $a = 1$, $b = 6$ and $c = 3$ years. Then the profit (%) from each of the three share types is:

$$x: \quad 5 + 30 + 15 = 50$$
$$y: \quad 20 - 30 = -10$$
$$z: \quad 10 + 30 = 40$$

so that one should buy x or z but not y (unless boom conditions are assured for a known period).

Selection of the best solution from a number of alternatives should be done with a quantitative basis, preferably using a process of summing *weighted attributes*.

A good example is the task of selecting the 'best' of three candidates Tom, Dick and Harry, for a job using the *decision table* of Table 14.1.

Here five attributes: qualifications, experience (relevant), age (or total experience), impression made at interview and strength of recommendations made by referees, are used and each of these is given a weight in the second column.

Then the three candidates are given a score out of ten for each attribute by each member of the selection panel and the results averaged (to the nearest round number for simplicity here), giving the results shown in columns 3,4,5.

Table 14.1.
Job candidate selection using weighted attribute scores.

Attribute	Weight	Score Tom	Dick	Harry	Weighted score Tom	Dick	Harry
Qualific-ations	2	8	5	3	16	10	6
Experience	3	5	7	6	15	21	18
Age	1	5	5	8	5	5	8
Interview	2	3	5	8	6	10	16
Referees	1	5	5	5	5	5	5
Total					46	51	53

Finally, these scores are multiplied by the weights, giving the results of columns 6, 7, 8 and these figures are summed to give the totals shown.

The final result indicates Harry as the best candidate.

In practice, however, it is best to include other considerations such as:

[1] Who top scored in the most important attributes?

[2] If the candidate is an existing employee (in another position) has there been any bias?

In this sort of analysis the choice of attributes is crucial, as is their weighting, so that such factors can also be reviewed before making a final decision.

Job seekers would do well, of course, to be aware of the decision-making process illustrated in Table 14.1, for example making a special effort to emphasize their previous work experience, especially *relevant* work experience, and also such factors as the *breadth, 'quality'* and *duration* of their work history, putting more emphasis on 'quality rather than quantity' of their qualifications and experience if they are younger applicants.

Decision trees

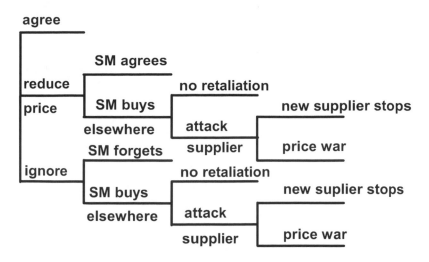

Figure 14.1. Example of a decision tree.

Decision trees are a useful way of depicting business strategies. A simple example is that of a manufacturer asked by a supermarket chain to make a 'home brand' version of its product, a decision tree for which is shown in Figure 14.1.

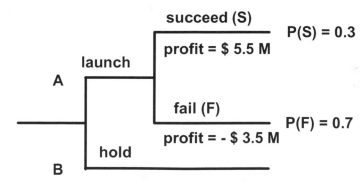

Figure 14.2. Decision tree with probabilities and financial outcomes.

As another example Figure 14.2 considers the problem of deciding whether to launch a rocket at a certain time or not, attaching probabilities and profit figures to the decision tree.

Then the Expected Monetary Value (EMV) of a launch is 0.3(5.5) - 0.7(3.5) = - $0.8M so we should decide to hold.

With more optimistic figures, for example P(S) = 0.7 and P(F) = 0.3, the EMV of **A** is $2.85M and the launch decision is much more favourable, though perhaps still not certain.

Conclusion

Decision trees, especially if they have probabilities and costs attached, are useful tools in the decision making process.

Decision tables are also useful, especially if they have weighted quantities to enable a total score to be given to the alternatives under consideration.

Mohr's Laws of Decisions are for the most part rudimentary, but nonetheless worth note. 'Don't rush', for example is very important and the basis of the cliché:

Err in haste, repent at leisure.

Similarly, getting a second (if not more) opinion and 'sleeping on it' are, of course, important. Board meetings of most organizations, for example, are typically monthly and run for two or three hours. Sometimes, however, there may be a long agenda and/or some important issues that require prolonged discussion and debate, and discussion of unresolved issues must be adjourned to a special meeting, or the next regular meeting.

In dealing with enthusiastic and 'pushy' sales persons, for example, one must be very careful, and trying to sell or buy a house can be a nightmare for 'ordinary' people. Auctions, in particular, cruelly force first home buyers to compete with experienced investors in a ridiculously hasty 'sidewalk show', often pressuring them into paying too high a price.

In such situations, of course, they need to have planned carefully in what area they want to live, how much they can afford to pay, what is a fair price they can limit themselves to paying, of course getting as much advice from friends or independent professional advisors as possible.

CHAPTER 15

DEALING WITH BAD BOSSES

I'm the boss. I'm allowed to yell.
Ivan Boesky, q. in *Den of* Thieves, James B Stewart, 1991.

*I asked why he was a priest and he said that
if you have to work for anybody an absentee boss is best.*
Jeanette Winterson, *The Passion,* ch. 1, 1987.

The Peter Principle

Dr Laurence Peter drew on his experiences in the education sector to try and explain why we always seem to have lousy leaders (Peter & Hull, 1969). The result was his celebrated *Peter Principle:*

IN A HIERARCHY EVERY EMPLOYEE TENDS TO RISE TO HIS OWN LEVEL OF INCOMPETENCE.

In other words, *the sour cream rises.*

A corollary is: *In time every post tends to be occupied by an employee who is incompetent to carry out his duties.*

In his often tongue-in-cheek book Peter gives a few excellent historical examples of his celebrated principle, including:

(a) Socrates was a brilliant philosopher but a lousy defence attorney.

(b) Hitler was a brilliant politician but a lousy general.

Mohr's Law of Hierarchies

This can illustrated by the small (hierarchical) DC network shown in Figure 15.1 which can be modelled as a DC network using a simple Finite Element Method program (Mohr, 1992, 2012a).

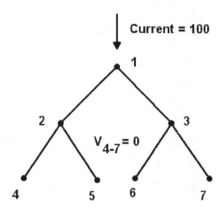

Figure 15.1. Hierarchical network.

At node 1 we have the pyramid building and lunatic 'boss' and a current 'load' of 100 is input. This is done by specifying the voltage at node 1 as 100, this being equivalent to adding a 'load' to the network.

Then zero datum voltage is specified at nodes 4-7 and unit resistance is given to all 6 elements so that the results from the program are:

Voltage 75 at node 1.

Voltage 25 at nodes 2 and 3.

Zero voltage at nodes 4 to 7.

Currents 50 in the top two elements and 25 in the rest.

This illustrates what the 'econobabble' of economists and politicians calls 'the trickle down effect', that is, the boss of this very small hierarchy has 3 times the voltage (or power, money and status) of his subordinates (the front line managers) one rung below. The workers at the bottom have no status at all.

132

If we add a further bottom row of 8 nodes in Figure 15.1 then now the 'voltage hierarchy' is 87.5, 37.5, 12.5, 0 so that the boss now does 7 times as well as the 'front line managers' on the row above the bottom row.

Then if we add a further fifth row of 16 nodes the voltage hierarchy is 93.75, 43.75, 18.75, 6.25, 0 and the boss does 15 times as well as the front line managers and infinitely better than the workers at the bottom!

The latter 'voltage hierarchy' is the fundamental principle of modern management, leading to Mohr's Law of Hierarchies:

In hierarchical organizations the amount of real material-producing work people do is inversely proportional to their rank or level in the organization. The amount of compensation they receive, however, is proportional to their level, sometimes to an exponential degree.

For such people their earnings might be expressed as an exponential function: $\$ = C \exp(kR)$

where $\$$ = salary, R = rank, and C and k are constants.

This, of course, is not fair at all.

In ancient times philosophers felt that nobody should be paid more than about 10 or 20 times as much as anybody else, and even that is a great difference, of course, but it might be justified in the case of an elected national leader who must be able to present a strong, powerful image and might have only a relatively short term in office.

In the case of big business, however, things have got out of hand and remuneration of CEOs is often tens of millions, on top of which they get huge share issues as annual bonuses, huge 'golden handshakes' when they retire, and gigantic 'golden parachutes' then the company collapses.

To add insult to the injury of poverty, the worker-slaves endure 'top-down one-way' (TDOW) communication as they did all through their long years at school, in other words, they are treated like shit.

This is grossly unjust as the poor peasants who work on farms, in factories or on building sites produce what is essential to human life, that is, food, clothing, housing etc.

So those posters often seen in the USSR decades ago which pictured the workers as heroic perhaps made some sense. Then, of course, the hammer and sickle on their flag was also symbolic of the importance of the workers.

So the bottom line is that we have to create fairer societies which have real or *direct democracy* and leaders who 'check their ego at the door'. In these greed, hunger, famine, war and other evils will not be tolerated by the people.

Power corrupts

As figure 15.1 illustrates, the higher up you are in a hierarchy the more 'power' you have, which might be stated symbolically as:

$$P = C R^n$$

where P = power, R = rank, and C and n are constants.

Assuming the value of n is 2 then when one is twice as high in the hierarchy one has four times as much power.

Then, as we all know, power corrupts, one of the major factors in mankind's endless history of conflict.

As noted in the previous section, salaries may increase exponentially in hierarchical organizations and this result can be related to Mohr's Law of Capitalism which is the exponential growth law of money ($) with time (T)

$$d(\$)/d(T) = c_1(\text{activity}) \quad \text{where activity} = c_2 \$$$

Here the rate at which money is made is proportional to the rate of business activity, this in turn proportional to the amount of money available to fund this activity.

Combining the two constants above as $k = c_1 c_2$ we have

$$d(\$)/d(T) = k\$ \quad \text{where } k \text{ is the } growth\ factor.$$

where $ = money made.

This is *separable* which means that it can be integrated in the form

Integral [d($)/$] = Integral [k d(T)]

giving, with the inclusion of the initial values, the exponential growth law $/$_0 = exp[k(T − T_0)]

If, for example, the growth factor is 10% per year, that is $k = 0.1$, then over 10 years we obtain the growth ratio $/$_0 = 2.7, so that we have nearly *tripled* our money.

The only real beneficiaries, however, are those higher in the hierarchy. The workers at the bottom who do all the *real work* (sitting and raving at sometimes boozy board meetings is not hard work) can't usually save any money and thus are slaves to all intents and purposes.

This is an intolerable situation and the CEOs who earn 'megabucks' are, of course, corrupt, and such corruption has always sown the seeds of discontent that have always, sooner or later, ended up as revolutions.

Thus socialism tends to be ruled by a single dictator, but capitalism by a multiplicity of petty dictators:

> *Capitalism tends to produce a multiplicity of petty dictators each in command of his own little business kingdom. State Socialism tends to produce a single, centralized totalitarian dictatorship, wielding absolute authority . . . through a hierarchy of bureaucratic agents.*
> Aldous Huxley, *Ends and Means* (1937).

Politicians too are often corrupt, of course, often being found to take bribes from big business.

Monarchs and dictators, of course, have nearly always been the greediest of all. Not only do they help themselves to plenty of money and live in grand palaces, but throughout history their hunger for power and thence territorial gain has led to one war after another.

How hierarchies operate

Hierarchies operate through a chain of command, leaders meeting with a chosen few top-level executives responsible for overseeing the various operations of the organization. In the case of government, for example, there are ministers for defence, treasury, education, health etc.

In each of these areas there are several levels of seniority ranging from head of the organization to department heads and front-line managers.

Through the whole chain of command there is an implicit level of intimidation and fear that usually makes sure that everybody does as they are told. At the front line, however, things often get ridiculous, for example the traditional screaming of army sergeants at their miserable subordinates.

It is through such bullying and intimidation, of course, that soldiers are brainwashed into following orders without question or delay, essentially becoming expendable slaves to satisfy the whims of their leaders. Don't worry about 'executive stress,' therefore, worry about 'slave-stress.'

Indeed, our many sports with a relationship to conflict, for example absurd rugby with its 'charge at the enemy' no matter what the risk of injury, or archery and rifle shooting, all relate to our historical predilection for conflict.

Throughout hierarchies there is ambition to rise, often leading to a good deal of competitive behaviour, much of it often downright dishonest. In politics, for example, plenty of 'backstabbing' goes on day in, and day out.

This corresponds quite closely, perhaps, with the alpha-male behaviour seen in several animal species, notably our close relatives, gorillas.

The problem, of course, is that people who have proved themselves good at the 'rat race', tend to be the worst leaders, exactly in accordance with the Peter Principle.

Not only that, power not only corrupts, it makes people vain, self-centred, neurotic, obsessive, and, basically, turns them into psychopaths.

Diagnosing psychopaths

Table 15.1. The Hare checklist for psychopaths.

	TRAIT	SCORE
	Facet 1: Interpersonal	
1	Glibness or superficial charm	1
2	Grandiose sense of self-worth	1
3	Pathological lying	2
4	Cunning or manipulative	1
	Facet 2: Affective	
5	Lack of remorse or guilt	1
6	Emotionally shallow	1
7	Callous or lack of empathy	1
8	Failure to accept responsibility for their own actions	1
	Facet 3: Lifestyle	
9	Need for stimulation (easily bored)	1
10	Parasitic lifestyle	1
11	Lack of realistic, long-term goals	0
12	Impulsivity	1
13	Irresponsibility	0
	Facet 4: Antisocial	
14	Poor behavioural controls	0
15	Early behavioural problems	0
16	Juvenile delinquency	0
17	History of conditional prison release being revoked	0
18	Criminal versatility	0
	Other traits:	
19	Many short-term marital relationships	0
20	Promiscuous sexual behaviour	0
TOTAL SCORE		**12**

In 1980, Canadian clinical psychologist Dr Robert Hare, who worked in prisons, released the first version of the Hare checklist for identifying psychopaths, and several further versions followed.

As shown in Table 15.1, it divides 20 personality traits into four groups: interpersonal, affective, lifestyle, and antisocial, these measuring traits including charm, propensity to lie, lack of remorse, and need for stimulation.

After an interview each trait is scored as 0 (not present), 1 (present but not dominant), or 2 (dominant), so that the maximum possible score is 40.

Average people score from 3 to 6, non-psychopathic criminals score from 16 to 22, whilst in the UK and US respectively, scores of >25 and >30 are taken as a positive diagnosis of psychopathy (Gillespie, 2017).

The first author has scored a couple of bad bosses he once had, both of whom were too young and inexperienced for being HOD, and played a major role in destroying his promising University career when he was less than 40.

Their total score of 12 seemed too low, as both seemed at least somewhat psychopathic, suggesting that Table 15.1 might apply more to hardened criminals for which item 17 relates to a form of 'treatment', namely continued imprisonment, presumably because of little or no sign of rehabilitation or remorse. Similarly, items 16 and 19 relate to past history.

Thus criteria for judging a bad boss should include:
➢ Bossiness.
➢ Assertiveness.
➢ Dishonesty and lying.
➢ Selfishness and greed.
➢ Vanity.
➢ Bullying.

Dealing with psychopaths

Gillespie (2017) suggests that organizations which are run using 'Management by Objectives' (MBO) are conducive to psychopathic bosses:

"The only way for a psychopath to succeed in a structure based on MBO would be to fall in with the objectives of his team and his superiors. Anything else would mark him out for removal from the organisation."

Alternatively, Gillespie suggests that persons deemed to be psychopaths can be got rid of by getting them 'fired', but this, of course, is very difficult to bring about when the only person in the part of the organization in question able to do firing is a psychopathic boss, as is often the case.

When you do go above his or her head seeking to get them fired they counterattack, usually resulting in the person or persons complaining being disciplined or fired.

Most workers, therefore, simply have to endure bad and mad bosses and a 2016 study of Australian workplaces with "toxic leaders" concluded that the following strategies were unwise (Gillespie, 2017):

➢ Confronting the leader.
➢ Avoiding, ignoring or bypassing the boss.
➢ Whistleblowing.
➢ Worrying to excess about the boss.
➢ Continued anger and frustration.
➢ Focussing on work to try and forget about the boss.
➢ Taking sick leave (giving only short-term relief).

Instead, Gillespie says one should behave as a polite and compliant employee and do whatever one is told, no matter how much one dislikes it. Then to survive in this way one should also:

➢ Think about a future, better job.
➢ Make sure your fellow workers don't 'tell' on each other.
➢ Check the accuracy of what the boss says.
➢ Don't show any anger and frustration.
➢ Build a support network.
➢ Document every bad thing the boss does, noting the time, date and names of any witnesses.

In this way one can survive for the medium term, at least, and perhaps build a case against the bad boss that might result in him being disciplined, demoted or shifted sideways, or even fired.

Conclusion

Hierarchies are difficult to deal with over the long term.

When one is young, and not long out of the education system, they are simply a learning experience at first. Over time, however, grudges over being treated badly, and impatience over lack of promotion, grow and grow to the point at which getting another job may seem the only hope of improving one's life and career prospects.

If one has a psychopathic 'bastard boss', however, it may be impossible to get a halfway supportive reference from them, without which getting a decent job, or any job at all in line with your abilities, qualifications and experience, may prove difficult.

In this way, indeed, just one bad boss can ruin your life, and in the first author's unfortunate case, two almost successive and too young/aggressive/alpha-male and inexperienced and boozing bastard bosses did, in fact, ruin his University career, as noted in Chapter One.

Some of the concepts and suggestions made in the foregoing chapter may be of some help, however, to workers with bad bass problems.

For example, remembering the Peter Principle will help one see the lighter side of the problem, while some of the suggestions made on how to diagnose and deal with psychopathic bosses might at least give the reader a few ideas from which he might be able to construct a strategy for dealing with a bad boss.

Primarily, of course, one needs at least one or two helpers within the organization in question. A problem here is that the workers at the same level in the hierarchy are also competing for the same promotion that you are. Thus, if you are in a group of, say, 10 seeking promotion to 'Senior xyz', then one might establish a mutually supportive relationship with just one of them, hoping that you will both be the next two workers promoted.

Chapter 16

Quality of Life

Life for the living, and rest for the dead.
The living need charity more than the dead.
George Arnold, *The Jolly Old Pedagogue* (1866).

Introduction

In speaking of quality of life it is difficult not to remember the cliché *quality is better than quantity,* but most people, of course would rather have both.

In the present chapter how to assess one's quality of life objectively is discussed. Study of the results can then suggest means by which one can improve one's life, perhaps by some of the means suggested in earlier chapters, for example solving existing problems, setting new goals and planning how to achieve them.

Life assessment

One can assess the quality of a particular aspect of one's life using the Expectation-Value and Information Integration methods of attitude assessment discussed in Chapter 7.

To assess the quality of several key aspects of one's life such methods as those discussed in Chapter 8 can be used, the simplest and most widely used of these being Likert Scaling.

Table 16.1 shows an example assessment for an adult person, scoring being done simply by using a printed copy of this table and circling the scores/ratings given to each of the items listed in the first column.

Table 16.1. Life quality questionnaire using Likert scaling.

Aspect of life: Circle the appropriate number	Very good	Good	Aver-age	Fair	Poor
Your work:					
1. Your job	5	4	3	2	1
2. Your pay	5	4	3	2	1
3. Relationship with boss	5	4	3	2	1
4. Workplace conditions	5	4	3	2	1
5. Relations with workmates	5	4	3	2	1
Your home life:	5	4	3	2	1
6. Your financial situation	5	4	3	2	1
7. Your home	5	4	3	2	1
8. Your parent(s) or partner	5	4	3	2	1
9. Your siblings or children	5	4	3	2	1
10. Your health	5	4	3	2	1
Recreation and social life:	5	4	3	2	1
11. Evening activities					
12. Weekend activities	5	4	3	2	1
13. Friends	5	4	3	2	1
14. Regular outings	5	4	3	2	1
15. Social, sport etc. groups	5	4	3	2	1
Your health:	5	4	3	2	1
16. General health	5	4	3	2	1
17. Fitness					
18. Diet	5	4	3	2	1
19. Weight					
20. Mental health	5	4	3	2	1
Add the numbers you circled:	**Score/100:**				

An 'average' rating of 3 on all 20 items gives, of course, a total score of 60. More important, perhaps, ratings of 1/poor for such important items as the first two (job and pay) might motivate one to try and improve these important life factors.

Similarly, a low rating for some of the health items might spur one into taking action to improve one's health.

In the wide range of items in Table 16.1 some items are much more important than others. Generally recreation and social life, for example, are not as important as one's job, and some jobs, of course, involve long hours 6 or 7 days a week, allowing little time for social life in any case.

Thus an evaluation such as that of Table 16.1 could be extended to include weights for each factor, as in the Information Integration method of attitude assessment discussed in Chapter 7, and this is done for the 'work' items of Table 16.1 in the following section.

Assessing a key aspect of life

One can assess the quality of a particular aspect of one's life using the Expectation-Value and Information Integration methods of attitude assessment discussed in Chapter 7.

As an example, we shall now assess the five 'work' items of Table 16.1 for a 'typical' person using the Information Integration method, giving the following result with weights and scores 1-10.

Attribute 1 (job): $w_1 = 5$, $s_1 = 5/10$ (i.e. 'halfway' values)

Attribute 2 (pay): $w_2 = 8/10$, $s_2 = 3/10$

Attribute 3 (relationship with boss): $w_3 = 7/10$, $s_3 = 4/10$

Attribute 4 (workplace conditions): $w_4 = 5/10$, $s_4 = 5/10$

Attribute 5 (relations with workmates): $w_5 = 4/10$, $s_5 = 5/10$

giving a total score

$= 5 \times 5 + 8 \times 3 + 7 \times 4 + 5 \times 5 + 4 \times 5$

$= 25 + 24 + 28 + 25 + 20 = 122$

whereas a 'middling evaluation score' with 5/10 for both the weights and scale values for all five items would give a total score of 125, so that the situation is perhaps 'satisfactory', for the present at least, but the low score of 3/10 for 'pay' is deserving of some attention sooner rather than later.

Planning life improvements

Having made the assessment of the preceding two sections, one may decide to address any issues raised by the only 'middling' score for the five work items obtained above. Though the 'pay' issue is the main concern, it is best to deal with all five work factors as doing so is more likely to improve the pay problem.

Table 16.2. Action plan re. job.

Item		Actions	Timing
1	Job	Stay Look for another job	1-2 years Now
2	Pay	Ask for a pay rise	Now
3	Boss	Talk to boss Make complaint	Next week In 3 months
4	Conditions	Talk to union Talk to boss	Next month In 3 months
5	Workmates	Meeting to raise issues	Next month

Table 16.2 illustrates an action plan to improve the work situation with one or two actions suggested for each of the five work items, including an approximate timing for each action.

Perhaps the key item is 1, where the plan is the cautious and sensible one of staying for a couple of years, but beginning to look for another job immediately – sensible because, of course, it can take a long time to find a job, and even longer to find a better one.

Most important, however, is that a simple plan such as this is far wiser than, for example, impatiently barging into the boss's office and abusing him about being underpaid, not an entirely unheard of situation.

Furthermore, having a sensible plan gives one hope for the immediate and medium term, as well as time to come up with other ideas to improve one's work situation, and to obtain help and advice from others on it.

Conclusions

Table 16.1 shows how one can make a quick assessment of the quality of one's life using simple Likert scaling.

The following section then uses the Information Integration method to assess a 'typical' person's job, Table 16.2 then suggesting actions to take on the five key factors of this important life issue. Then, of course, the same approach can be used to examine other aspects of one's life, and decide upon actions to improve those aspects, including a timeframe for those actions.

As for quality of home life, in an article in Melbourne's Herald-Sun newspaper on 28/8/17 it was reported that a group of six "oldies" said that they thought such basic things as a sound diet, plenty of exercise, quality relaxation time, and a good social life to be the key to better health and happiness in old age.

An appropriate bottom line here, however, is that, as a job network lady interviewing the first author once told him when he was talking about past problems:

You can't change the past.

This, of course, is very true – but one can change one's future and improve it by such simple means as those discussed in the foregoing chapter, and elsewhere in this book.

As for the usefulness of 'occupational therapy', a good example might be such politicians as Al Gore who, after narrowly failing to become President of the USA, took an interest in the issue of climate change, eventually winning a Nobel Prize for his efforts. Others might be former Victorian Premier Jeff Kennett, and former Australian Prime Minister Julia Gillard, who became successive CEOs of the phone counselling service Beyond Blue.

CHAPTER 17

INVENTING A NEW RELIGION

*The concept of "God" invented as a counter-concept
of life – everything harmful, poisonous, slanderous,
the whole hostility unto death against life synthesized
in the concept of a gruesome entity!*
Friedrich Nietzsche, *Ecco Homo* (1888).

Religion has always been the wound, not the bandage.
Dennis Potter (1935 – 1994), British playwright,
Observer, London, April 10, 1994: 'Sayings of the Week.'

*Men never do evil so completely and cheerfully
as when they do it from religious conviction.*
Blaise Pascal (1623 – 1662), *Pensées* (1669), no. 894.

Inventing religions

Primitive man's earliest religions developed as a way of comprehending a bewilderingly complex world. It was perhaps 'natural' to ascribe one's thinking to an inner spirit, and then assume other objects also had spirits. Some primitive tribes believed in a supreme spirit or god, and eventually monotheism evolved, most notably in Judaism.

By this time religion had evolved a good deal and the practice of inventing religious fables had become part and parcel of every culture, religious rituals being one of relatively few ways of passing spare time.

With the coming of the Agricultural Revolution communities grew in size and, with hunter-gathering no longer obligatory for all men, occupations were able to diversify to include community leaders, priests and soldiers.

147

Specialist priests, of course, needed to develop stories of their religion to be taught as folklore, these often being a mix of tribal history in which many events are attributed to gods.

The Hebrew folklore that formed the Jewish scriptures told the history of the Jewish people, much of the book of Genesis telling of 'creation', the history of the first Jewish people, and how they ended up enslaved in Egypt.

With the appearance of Moses, the self-appointed leader claiming communications from God, we see the same sort of story that shamans had always told. The book of Exodus, however, marks the real beginning of the Jewish faith as we know it today.

Today, however, there are only about 20 or 30 million Jews. Christianity, an extension of Judaism, however, reportedly has some 2 billion followers. Then Islam, an extension of Christianity, has some 1.2 billion followers.

It seems, therefore, that the story of Jesus might well be, as has sometimes been said, the 'greatest story ever told.' He was not a poor preacher, but from the house of David and he had a number of siblings, at least some of them born to his mother Mary who was therefore certainly not a virgin in the long run, nor when she bore Jesus.

Indeed, the entire story of Jesus in the Bible reeks with conspiracy, for example a voice from heaven pronouncing him the son of God when he is baptized at age 30 by John the Baptist, Mary's cousin.

At that point then, the plan had been hatched, and Jesus finds his first four disciples by the Sea of Galilee.

The script for the crucifixion may have then come from the book of Zechariah, namely the messiah riding into Jerusalem on an ass, his hands being wounded because of his friends, his body being pierced, and then mourned in death by all of Jerusalem (Gardner, 2001).

That Jesus might be crucified for his preaching, preaching that the Romans were certain to see as likely to result in insurrection, was foreseeable. Indeed, he virtually forecast this outcome at the Last Supper, and then encouraged it by refusing to defend himself when tried by the Roman authorities.

When men were crucified they usually took days to die, often a week or more. Often, therefore, the process was sped up by breaking their legs to place more weight on their arms, their hands being nailed. Jesus, however, only lasted a few hours until he was given, according to Matthew 27:34, "vinegar mixed with gall" or soured wine mixed with snake venom. This was, according to Gardner (2001), administered by Simon Zelotes via a sponge to which some of the mixture had been added by a reed, thus ensuring that the dose was small enough to render Jesus unconscious without killing him.

Originally Simon Zelotes was meant to be one of the three men crucified, but according to Gardner (2001):

The Islamic Koran (chapter 4, entitled Women) specifies that Jesus did not die on the cross, stating: 'Yet they slew him not, neither crucified him, but he was represented by one in his likeness . . . They did not really kill him.' Also, the 2nd-century historian, Basilides of Alexandria, wrote that the crucifixion was stage-managed (with Simon the Cyrene used as a substitute), while the gnostic leader, Mani (born near Baghad in AD214), made precisely the same assertion.

Simon Zelotes, indeed, was well qualified to mastermind the hoax of the crucifixion, being Head of the Samaritan Magi and the greatest magician of his day. Thus, while the crosses were being erected, he changed places with Simon the Cyrene, who, therefore seems to have been the real martyr that day (Gardner, 2001).

Rendered unconscious by the small dose of poisoned vinegar, Jesus was speared by a soldier and bled, indicating that he was alive according to Dr A. R. Kittermaster's 1979 report *A Medical View of Calvary* (Gardner, 2001).

Because the unconscious Jesus showed no response to this injury, however, he was presumed dead by the guards who broke the legs of the other two men to hasten their death.

Then Joseph of Arimathea, actually Jesus' eldest brother James the Less, was the man who, on the basis of religious arguments, was allowed to take Jesus from the cross and put him in a family sepulchre which had two connected chambers (Gardner, 2001).

Then, of course, Jesus would have awoken before long and probably left the tomb on the Saturday, if not earlier. The next day he was seen near the tomb by his mother, and Mary Magdalene, his wife, and he told them to tell his disciples to meet him in Galilee.

A remarkable hoax that the Koran sees as such, but then seeks to upstage with Muhammad claiming to be God's final prophet of a day of final judgment. The Koran, however, also involves a tale of resurrection, namely the awaited reappearance of the 12th Imam, the Mahdi, to rule in the last years before the Day of Judgment, and to be accompanied by no other than Jesus Christ.

The Koran makes it clear, however, that Christ was not the son of God, saying in 19.88:

Those who say: 'The Lord of Mercy has begotten a son,' preach a monstrous falsehood, at which the very heavens might crack, the earth split asunder, and the mountains crumble to dust.

With such a history of disagreement and violent conflict between the two religions, it should be considered that, if Christianity is an extension of Judaism, and then Islam an extension of Christianity, then why should this be the end of the story?

In the rest of this chapter, therefore, one final addition to the countless religious texts that still abound is made, hoping that it will provide a more realistic view of life for generations to come.

Mohronism

Mohronism is one of the newest religions. It was launched by the (limited) publication of the book *Mohr's Laws, What Went Wrong With You and the World and What To Do About It* (Mohr, 2003). Unfortunately few copies of this book are extant now. This book holds that the Real Truth is that Murphy was God's prophet, this being Mohr's 9th Law (Mohr, 2003, 2012b), explaining why, throughout history, mankind has lurched from one disaster to another and is now threatened with extinction, not salvation (Mohr, 2012c).

And who pray tell is Murphy? He was the celebrated Murphy of Murphy's law, credited to the eponymous Edward Murphy who in 1948, when strain gauges failed to work on a sled on rails carrying a chimpanzee to test the effect of 'g' forces on the body at the now named Edwards Air Force Base, blamed his assistant, saying something along the lines: *"If that guy has any way of making a mistake, he will."*

Team discussions then modified this to:

"Anything that can go wrong, will go wrong"

and named it for Murphy.

In charge of the tests was Dr John Stapp, who published a collection of aphorisms and adages in 1992. In his first press conference about the project he referred to Murphy's Law which soon spread widely. Stapp is credited with Stapp's Law:

"The universal aptitude for ineptitude makes any human accomplishment an incredible miracle" (Wikipedia, 2013).

The bottom line, of course, is that in mankind's ongoing history of one disaster after another, everything does indeed go wrong usually. Occasionally, something good happens, for example the discovery of penicillin, but that too was an accident resulting from 'bugs' from a lab whose door had been mistakenly left open overnight invading a Petri dish in another lab. The next morning it was discovered that a mould in that dish had prevented multiplication of bacteria.

Murphy's God, indeed, must have been the person who so many writers of religious fables and creeds had visions of, and who commanded them to write such drivel as is found in almost all religious texts.

They should be converted from insanity to Mohronism, and to believing that, indeed, Murphy was God's prophet. We can even give you his phone number but have forgotten it right now, just when we need it. Even when we do remember it, however, we only get his answering machine on the line with the message:

I can't get to the phone right now because I've lost it.

As a bottom line, therefore, anyone offended by anything we have said should not blame us. Why not pray tell? Because Murphy's God is to blame for anything that goes wrong, including anything that we've said that might be deemed by some to be wrong for, indeed, we were, of course, only trying to tell the truth and therefore shine a light on the truth.

Furthermore, anyone so inclined should beware of having a fatwa issued about us, or placing a curse on us. Even if you do, you see, in all probability Murphy's God will make sure it backfires and comes back to haunt you.

Table 17.1 shows all 10 Mohr's Laws, most of which we shall not elaborate upon much at this point, leaving that to those that follow. Briefly then, the laws are:

[1] The first law is that there are three human personality types: placid, neutral, and aggressive (Mohr, 2012b).

[2] The second concerns itself with the brainwashing we are subjected to throughout life, whether by education, religion, political propaganda, or ubiquitous modern advertising.

[3] The third concerns the increasingly 'boxed in' nature of the lives of we troglodytes who spend most of our time cooped up in a room, car, tram, or train.

Table 17.1. Table of Mohr's Laws

Law #	Law name	Subject	Principle
1	Mohr's morphology	human personality	three basic personality types
2	Mohr's mentation	education etc.	brainwashing
3	Mohr's metamorphosis	home, pub & coffin	life in three boxes
4	Mohr's mirage	sex	myth of love
5	Mohr's malady	hierarchy & power	law of the 'rat race'
6	Mohr's mechanism	achievement	madness required
7	Mohr's motto	power	power corrupts
8	Mohr's misery	crime & war	human condition
9	Mohr's mantra	man's history	the prophet Murphy
10	Mohr's metrology	final judgment	?/9

[4] The fourth law is that sex is God's joke on mankind, we being too stupid to realize this (Mohr & Fear, 2015).

[5] The fifth concerns the law of hierarchies discussed in Chapter 15:

In hierarchical organizations the amount of real material-producing work people do is inversely proportional to their rank or level in the organization. The amount of compensation they receive, however, is proportional to their level, sometimes to an exponential degree.

[6] The sixth law is that 'madness' is required to achieve anything important. The 'mad scientist' is an example where a typical Murphy-type contradiction appears: the scientist who makes an important discovery is rarely mad, but exceptionally sensible. Thus we defined *sad mad, bad mad,* and *good mad* in Chapter 9, the mad scientist falling into the latter category.

[7] The seventh law is that power corrupts, as all history shows, and this needs little elaboration. Indeed, there are aspects of Transactional Analysis (TA) here, as people made boss usually do, indeed, undergo a change of behaviour for the worse.

[8] The eighth law laments the misery of the pathetic human condition, and thus man's never-ending history of mistakes, including crime and war. Indeed, that we have bred like animals so that our survival is now threatened, like that of so many other species, is testimony to our stupidity (Mohr, 2012b).

[9] As already noted, the ninth law is that we are governed by the law of the Prophet Murphy. We thought we had better mention this again, however, in case you had forgotten.

[10] The final law is that 10, or perfection, is impossible, and 0 is impossibly bad, for example, in the case of health (or how much alive one is) zero would be dead. Thus there are only 9 possible scores by which to judge people. The really important point here, however, is that no issue of any complexity is 'simply black and white'. Generally, therefore, we should judge things on the Mohr Scale of one to nine (Mohr, 2003; Mohr & Fear, 2015).

The first corollary to Murphy's Law is: *If anything can go wrong, it will, and at the worst possible time.*

There are countless other Murphy's Laws and a book on project scheduling called *The Pertatorium* had a list of 100 of them along the lines of:

➢ *The first 90% of the job takes 90% of the time, the last 10% takes the other 90%.*
➢ *When you throw out the instructions and warranty for an appliance, it is then that it will break down.*
➢ The law of selective gravity: *An object will fall so as to do the most damage.*

17. Inventing a New Religion

Bearing in mind that Christianity was not accepted as the official religion in Rome until 380 AD, we will not guess how long the new religion that Murphy was God's prophet (Mohronism) will take to be accepted by more than a handful of people.

When disciples of the prophet Murphy do get around to writing the Bible of Mohronism we hope it is filled with outlandish claims, dire predictions, and repetition and mistakes, just as other religious texts are, and in accordance with Murphy's Law which, of course, governs all religions.

We doubt that great churches like the 6th century Hagia Sophia in Constantinople will be built to celebrate Mohronism, however, and its worshippers might have to make do with natural places of worship or erected stones (menhirs) as the Celts and other peoples did. In fact, those worshipping the prophet Murphy might do well to 'get stoned' in the current Australian colloquial sense, not in the sense that Matthias, the apostle chosen to replace Judas Iscariot did, that is, being stoned before being beheaded. If Murphy's disciples do get drunk, however, we should not like them to 'loose their head' as Matthias did in anything but the colloquial sense.

Mohronism should have, of course, some sort of 'power sign' to replace the Christian one of 'crossing oneself'. Bearing in mind Mohr's 9th Law, this cannot be Winston Churchill's famous 'V for victory' sign. Nor can it be raising the index and little fingers, which supporters of the Texas Longhorn football team understand as representing the horns of a bull, but which Italian men take to mean that you are going to bed with their wife (Pease, 2004).

The sign we propose for Mohronism is made by touching one's thumb and forefinger together to form an 'O', thus representing a circle, an object to which traditional North American religions attach much importance. This sign could also be taken to represent Mohr's Circle, which is much used in the study of the engineering mechanics of stresses.

155

We hope the Mohron Church will not give scientists a bad time, as the Christian Church did Copernicus and Galileo, Martin Luther calling the former "a fool who went against the Holy Writ", whilst we all know at least a little of the trial of Galileo and his being sentenced by the Catholic Church to life imprisonment (in fact he served time under house arrest because of his being 70 at the time).

Better that than going to a Catholic School and being abused, however, by a priest!

Catholicism is, of course, the strictest Christian sect (of many), and therefore, it follows, also the most hypocritical.

The same applies to the strictest, most rabid, Muslim sect, the Wahhabi sect that Osama Bin Laden belonged to.

Finally, remember that Murphy's God is a benevolent God, not an evil one like most others who repeatedly promise dire vengeance on countless people, as one reads in so many parts of the Bible.

When things always go wrong, you see, it is always our fault, and Murphy's Law is based on our behaviour, not his. If, indeed, we followed Mohr's laws, we would be much better off. For example:

> Aware of the 9th law, we might be more careful and not rush into things.
> If we followed the 10th law, we would not be so prejudiced and inclined to fight over minor differences between people such as hogwash religions, and instead we would make more measured judgments. We should not merely have friends or enemies, for example, but rate people on the Mohr scale of 0 to 9.
> The other 8 laws should give us a better understanding of the human condition and how to cope with it.

Finally, is there to be some end of world scenario according to Mohronism? This is discussed in the recent book *The Doomsday Calculation* (Mohr, 20121c), the quotation which opens Chapter One being:

In 1956 Professor W.A. Lewis calculated that if the world population were to double every 25 years (a rate of increase currently observable in some parts of Africa and Asia), it would reach 173,500 thousand million by the year 2330, at which time there would be standing room only, since this is the number of square yards on the land surface of the earth.
John Carey, *The Faber Book of Science* (1995),
'The Menace of Population.'

Finally, note that, according to Mohr's 10th law, your overall score on anything can never be more than 9/10, so that, in fact, things only go wrong 9 times out of ten.

This is certainly more rational than, for example, the Jews claiming to be the chosen people amongst all others.

Indeed, at a time when most religions are on the wane, it is hoped that the new religion Mohronism will gain millions of followers and be followed with the same fervour that, for example, fans of British Premier League teams show.

For example, the Australian Football League star Gary Ablett was often referred to as 'God' or 'The Pontiff' by fans, with good reason according to another former AFL star, Doug Hawkins (1995).

Finally, if reading this chapter convinces a few people of the folly of religion, then that would be a good thing.

If, on the other hand, this chapter convinces people that they should become Mohrons, then we would ask them not to resort to conflict and violence on account of their new faith.

Conclusions

Mohronism has no son of God such as JC, so there can be no great schism in the Mohron Church such as occurred over the *filioque*, that is, whether the Holy Spirit proceeds from the Father, or both the Father and the Son.

Note too that Murphy's God arises out of ontological, not cosmological thinking. The Universe always existed in some form or other (Mohr, Sinclair & Fear, 2014), it is simply Mohr's 9th Law that mankind has usually followed the prophet Murphy's Law throughout mankind's disastrous history.

Finally, it is left to disciples, of whom it is hoped there will be many, to spread the word of the prophets Murphy and Mohr (Mohr & Fear, 2015).

One appropriate way of doing this would be in the manner of the stylites, of whom there were many in the century following the death of St Simeon Stylites in 459AD.

As a bottom line on the new religion Mohronism, followers should note that at the commencement of celebrations (a BYO party) one should bring something broken as a votive sacrifice, broken pottery, for example, as did ancient Egyptian worshippers if they were poor. The prophet Murphy would be pleased, of course, to see something else had gone wrong.

For special occasions the most rabid supporters of Mohronism could be exhibited in like fashion to the regular Sunday exhibitions of lunatics at the Bethlehem madhouse in England which continued until 1815. These shows made a good deal of money and are immortalized in the English language by the word 'Bedlam' which is a contraction of Bethlehem (Youngson & Schott, 1996).

Mohronism does not require baptism, but, in cases of advancing age, a brain transplant, this new 'awakening' being accompanied by substantial Mohronist brainwashing.

Finally, Sod's Law should be mentioned as some statements of this are equivalent to Murphy's Law. It derives, perhaps, from the expression "unlucky sod" for a person with bad luck.

O'Toole's commentary on Murphy's Law, namely: *Murphy was an optimist,* should also be noted. Indeed, Mohrons are optimists as they always hope that, eventually, something will go right, not wrong.

In this context Barth's Distinction is relevant:

There are two types of people: those who divide people into two types and those who do not.

This relates to Mohr's Law of Politics, that is:

When we build a political 'fence' of some kind then people will generally divide fairly equally on both sides of it.

Mohr's 10th Law, however, seeks to remedy this, advising that we rate all issues on the Mohr Scale, and readers are asked to rate Mohronism and other religions on that scale.

Finally, ending this book, we should point out that, whilst the prophet of Mohronism, Murphy, and his celebrated law, may seem pessimistic and inappropriate in a book about hope, it does indeed summarize human history with great accuracy. As for the future, however, we should HOPE that things will improve and that mankind can begin to effectively tackle the problems that threaten his very existence such as overpopulation, continuing conflict and global Islamic jihad, resource depletion, pollution, and global warming and thus avoid extinction (Mohr, 2012b).

As for final judgements, Mohr's 10th Law should always be borne in mind, and it should be noted that it can, indeed, give a more measured and optimistic view of things because when things go wrong they are not 'written off' as a total disaster or lost cause, etcetera, but scored as perhaps just a poor result of, say, 2/10, and we can then HOPE that given time and effort we can improve the situation and score.

17. Inventing a New Religion

CHAPTER 18

CONCLUSIONS

He who does not hope to win has already lost.
José Juaquin Olmedo, (1780-1847), attrib.

True hope is swift, and flies with swallows' wings.
William Shakespeare, *Richard III*, act 5, sc. 2, 1.23 (1592-3).

Introduction

As discussed in Chapter 1, the evolution of homo sapiens sapiens brought the gift of advanced language that sets him apart from other animal species. With it came religion to try and explain the complex world surrounding him, and to try and control the animal instincts and behaviours that persisted. Sadly, however, we have a deplorable history of conflict inherited from the apes from whom we evolved, a history made worse by the invention of increasingly sophisticated and deadly weapons.

Despite the myriad problems of natural disaster, disease, and conflict over territory, resources and ethnicity, mankind's population has exploded, particularly since the Industrial Revolution of only about a couple of hundred years ago.

Hope and optimism, however, have played a great part in mankind's progress from primitive troglodytes to advanced technological societies, thanks to over a thousand years of increasingly widespread, complex and effective scientific thought and research.

As discussed in Chapter 2, therefore, it is important that our young are encouraged by parents, teachers and others to grow up with the hope, optimism and enthusiasm that will help make their lives happier and more productive.

Religion

Chapter 1 briefly noted how, early in history, tribal witch doctors or shamans propounded superstitious and sectarian views that encouraged tribal conflict.

Chapter 3 discussed religion in more detail, giving several examples of how religions were invented by Moses, Zoroaster, Christ, Buddha, Muhammad etcetera, resulting in a proliferation of religions that continued in the 20th century.

There has not only been conflict between religions throughout the centuries, but some of the most bitter conflicts have been between religious sects over seemingly minor details, perhaps the most notable examples being between Catholics and Protestants during The Reformation, and the bitter conflict between Sunnis and Shiites that continues to this day.

Chapter 3 gives just a few examples of religious corruption, ranging from 'extracting' money from people with a profusion of lies to the widespread sexual abuse in the Catholic Church that dates back centuries, and to the now global Islamic jihad of recent decades that some view as "World War 3" (Mohr, Fear & Sinclair, 2015).

Hope improves life

Chapter 4 notes a study of 800 people that found that those more "hopeful" had better lives and lived longer.

Then hope and optimism, goal creation, and the importance of leadership with "compassion, stability, trust, and hope" were discussed, an important example being the well-known *teacher expectancy effect.*

The sorts of things we should hope for, and how to deal with problems when things go wrong were then discussed.

Chapter 5 discussed the importance of motivational leadership, good management communication, workgroup loyalty, positive and optimistic attitudes, and conflict avoidance in the workplace in improving morale and productivity.

The psychology of attitudes

Chapter 6 discussed various types of advertising and how these target both basic needs such as for food and clothing, and *metaneeds* such as beauty, status and wealth.

Political and religious propaganda were also discussed, along with the important issue of to what extent is ubiquitous modern advertising and propaganda 'brainwashing' that reduces us to "consumer zombies".

Chapter 7 discussed the very useful Reception-Yielding model of attitude formation, learning and forgetting curves, and *mere exposure research*.

Also discussed were the expectancy-value and information integration models of attitude formation which use algebraic summation of scale values of various attributes to obtain an overall assessment of attitude towards an object.

Chapter 8 detailed four methods of measuring attitudes:
1. Thurston's method of equal-appearing intervals.
2. Likert's method of summated ratings.
3. Guttman scaling.
4. Bogardus' social stimulus scale.

and Likert scaling proves useful in Chapter 16 to assess 'quality of life'.

Psychology and psychiatry

Chapter 9 briefly discusses the history of psychiatry and then outlines the main psychological disorders, including mania, depression, anxiety, OCD, hypochondria, Tourette's syndrome, Asperger's syndrome, autism, ADHD, dyslexia, schizophrenia, psychosis, hysteria, dementia, homosexuality, and PTSD.

The chapter concludes with the 3 simple categories of madness:
1. Sad mad: e.g. depression, anxiety and OCD.
2. Bad mad: e.g. psychopaths and bullying, lying etc.
3. Good mad: e.g. "mad" scientists, outlandish artists etc.

18. Conclusions

The psychology of habits

Chapter 10 discussed the psychology of habits, beginning with Piaget's 'accommodation' by which infants become accustomed to their surroundings, and moving on to imitative and social learning which play an important role both in childhood and later life.

The effects of religious and political propaganda, the mass media, and advertising are then discussed, these being responsible for many lifelong habits, for example, the religions and political persuasions we follow.

The 'bad habits' are discussed, including a range of psychopathic behaviours and addictions, including, for example, bullying and lying, and addiction to gambling and drugs.

It is then suggested that we should develop 'good habits' that improve our lives and health, including positive thinking and goal setting, for example trying to get a promotion or better job, or trying to improve our home lives with healthier diet, daily exercise, and plenty of relaxation.

The psychology of conflict

Chapter 11 briefly discussed the well-known 'contact hypothesis' which relates ethnic differences between two groups of people to their cultural differences and the amount of contact between them, 'negative contact' or conflict, of course, increasing the ethnicity of the two groups.

This is extended by Mohr's attitudinal model of conflict which takes the simple form:

$$A^* = A + xB + yC + zD$$

where A^* = current 'overall' attitude,
A = initial or 'basic' attitude (based on 'known history'),
B = attitude towards behaviours of the second party,
C = contact history between the two parties,
D = degree of difference between the parties considered,
and x, y, z are scaling factors that indicate the relative importance of the terms they are associated with.

An example application of this model is then given, and it is also extended to include the effect on group attitude of 'societal views', and attitudes towards responses that might be made to deal with a second conflicting/opposing group.

Several other factors that effect group attitudes and conflict are then discussed, for example economic factors and proximity.

The chapter concludes by noting that man's disastrous history of conflict is unlikely to end because of overpopulation, resource depletion, economic problems etc., suggesting that *real democracy* might improve our prospects, Mohr defining this as a parliament of freely elected representatives for each electorate who are not aligned to a political party, but truly independent in representing the people of their electorate, and not some hierarchical and thus usually corrupt party (Mohr, 2012b).

Psychological treatment

Chapter 12 introduced Eysenck's three dimensions or 'supertraits' of psychoticism, extraversion/introversion and neuroticism, and Gillespie's three categories of psychological behaviours: schizophrenic, dramatic, and anxious.

Such classifications, of course, allow one to approximately begin psychological assessment of a person.

Then several alternative treatments for psychological disorders are noted, including 'talk therapy', 'motivational interviewing', 'transference' counselling for PTSD, hypnosis, prescription drugs, cognitive behavioural therapy, group therapy meetings, mindfulness meditation, 'chat groups' etc. at local council community centres, and support organizations such as Rainbows (Marta, 2004).

Building self-confidence and hope

Chapter 13 discussed developing self-esteem, self-confidence, self-reliance, self-regulation, self-assessment, creative and positive thinking, and goal-setting, giving a tabular example of a person's assessment of their life.

Planning for success

Chapter 14 discussed the 3 stages of:
(a) Creative thinking via preparation, incubation, and assembly.
(b) Problem solving via definition of the problem, generating possible solutions, and testing and evaluating these alternative solutions.

Then lateral thinking to find less obvious alternative solutions and Mohr's 10 simple laws of decisions were discussed.

Finally the important tools of decision tables and decision trees were discussed.

Dealing with bad bosses

Chapter 15 began by noting the important Peter Principle of hierarchies, along with Mohr's Law of Hierarchies, giving a simple DC network example of the latter, and Mohr's Law of Capitalism, which shows how the wealth of some people and organizations can exponentiate with time.

The issues of how power corrupts and how bosses tend to become greedy, vain, self-centred, neurotic, and obsessive psychopaths are then discussed.

Then how to rate psychopaths on the Hare checklist for psychopaths is demonstrated, concluding with a simple and more practical list of criteria for judging a bad boss, the chapter concluding with discussion of the how to deal with psychopathic bosses, an important issue for many downtrodden workers in large and hierarchical organizations.

Quality of life

Chapter 16 showed how to use Likert scaling to examine the quality of one's life in detail.

Then the Information Integration method was used to assess the five 'work' items of the quality of life assessment using fairly 'typical' scores, and this result used to develop an action plan to improve the 'work' aspect of life.

166

Then, in like fashion, of course, one can examine and improve other aspects of one's life.

When quality of life is minimal, for example being bedridden with a terminal disease or just very old age, many people consider euthanasia, now legalized somewhat in a growing number of countries. For this purpose such drugs as Nembutal, which are freely available on the Internet, are often used. In Australia, however, Nembutal is increasingly likely to be confiscated by customs.

Inventing a new religion

Chapter 17 discussed how the concepts of spirits and gods were developed by primitive man, and how ever since countless religions have been 'invented' by unscrupulous men seeking status, political power, and wealth.

How Christianity, and then Islam, were developed as extensions of Judaism is then discussed, paying particular attention to perhaps the greatest hoax in history, the crucifixion of Jesus Christ, in which, of course, he did not die, but the legend of his supposedly being the son of God grew into one of the world's most widespread religions.

To give the world real HOPE, therefore, the new religion of Mohronism is proposed and its 10 laws are presented and discussed, principal amongst these being:

(a) The 9th law is that the prophet of Mohronism is Murphy, whose celebrated law sums up mankind's mostly disastrous history of ignorance and conflict very well.

(b) The 10th law is that all judgements should be made numerically on the Mohr Scale of 0 – 9, so that important issues are not simply judged as 'black and white', or 'good and bad'.

In the context of HOPE, the latter law is of great importance, for example, when things go wrong (as they usually do according to Murphy) we should not quickly give up, but rather score a bad outcome as say, only 2, and then HOPE and plan to get better results.

Conclusion

Finally, to conclude on a positive note, we believe that it is important in life to have HOPE for, when one looses all hope, life will seem not worth living. Thus students thrive on encouragement and hope, as exemplified by the 'teacher expectancy effect', whilst people suffering from depression can be helped greatly if they are given HOPE.

Mankind's disastrous history of conflict seems unlikely to end and we face other threats as a result of overpopulation, resource depletion, climate change etcetera. The authors HOPE we can solve some of these problems, however, and thus increase our chances of avoiding the extinction forecast for many animal species, including ourselves.

As noted in earlier chapters of the present book, we should push for *real democracy,* as outlined in Chapter 20 of *The Doomsday Calculation* (Mohr, 2012b), rather than the highly oligarchical and antiquated Westminster system that still governs much of the Western world today, and only then, perhaps, might there be any real chance of avoiding increasing global catastrophes and perhaps extinction as a result of overpopulation etc. or nuclear and biochemical warfare (Mohr, 2012c).

Finally, we hope that the new religion Mohronism will find increasing and everlasting support both in heaven and earth. Then mankind can use its 9th law to positive effect by realizing the phrase *everything that can go wrong will go wrong* should encourage us to plan things (including our lives) more intelligently and carefully so that there are as few as possible *things that can go wrong.*

We HOPE, therefore, that some of the discussion, concepts and methods presented in this book will help readers to make better judgements using the Mohr Scale and use optimism and HOPE to set goals and make plans to make their lives, and the world we live in, better.

APPENDIX

POKER MACHINE PROGRAM

Chapter 10 discussed the psychology of habits, including gambling, noting the similarity of poker machines to Skinner boxes in which rats quickly learn to press a lever to obtain a food reward. The millions of people around the world addicted to 'pokies', of course, HOPE to make a profit which they occasionally do. In the long run, of course, they almost invariably lose. The simple BASIC program given here, however, can be played at no cost so one cannot lose, but nor can one win either. One will loose/waste time, however, and that is also an important consideration.

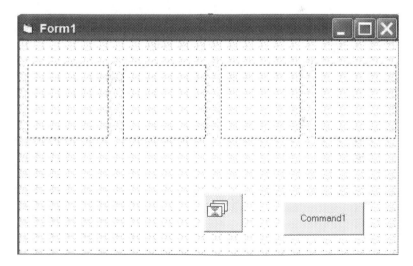

The 'Form' pokie.frm for a simple Visual Basic 5 poker machine program pokie.vbp is shown above. Four pictures are stored in the 'Image List' attached to the form to the left of the 'Command1' button.

The simple coding (pokie.vbp) for the program is:

```
Private Sub Command1_Click()
Dim i, k, c, s, j(4)  As Integer
s = 0
For k = 1 To 4
x = Rnd: y = 4 * Rnd: i = Int(y) + 1
s = s + i: j(k) = i
Set Image1(k - 1).Picture = ImageList1.ListImages(i).Picture
Next
c = 0: For k = 1 To 4: If j(k) = s / 4 Then c = c + 1
Next
a$ = "1"
If c = 4 Then a$ = InputBox("FOUR", , , 4000, 4000)
i = CInt(a$)
If i = 0 Then End
End Sub
```

To play the game one selects 'Run' from the Visual Basic menu, then pressing the Command1 button to fill the four 'Image' boxes on the form, as shown below.

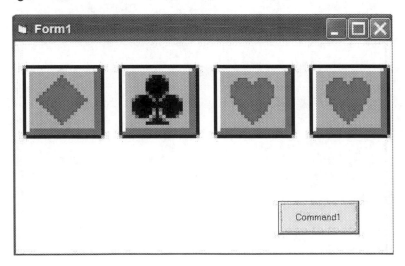

One then keeps pressing the command button until all four images are of the same suite.

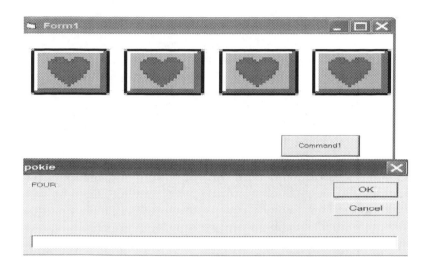

When this happens an 'Input Box' appears, as shown above, and one must then type any integer number but zero to continue the game, or zero to end it.

Most readers will, of course, be unfamiliar with Visual Basic, but perhaps the foregoing example will at least give them some idea of how it works.

More important, however, this simple program will perhaps illustrate the trivial nature of poker machines, and without the 'bells and whistles' and clatter of money occasionally dropping out of other machines in the gambling venue, this simple game is certainly not addictive, and not likely to be played for more than a couple of minutes until one sees how it works by getting 'four of same suite' once or twice.

Readers interested in simple programming will find an introduction to BASIC programming and several useful QBASIC programs in the first author's recent book *The Scientific MBA* (Mohr, 2017).

Appendix

REFERENCES

Anthony, R (Dr), *The Ultimate Secrets of Total Self-Confidence, Master the Simple Step-by-step principles and change your life,* John Blake, London (2010).

Arkowitz H, Miller WR, Rollnick S, *Motivational Interviewing in The Treatment of Psychological Problems,* The Guilford Press, New York (2015).

Atrens D, Curthoys I, *The Neurosciences and Behaviour: An Introduction,* 2nd edn, Academic Press, Sydney (1982).

Ben-Menashe A, *Profits of War, The Sensational Story of the World-Wide Arms Conspiracy,* Allen & Unwin, Sydney (1992).

Butler-Bowden, Tom, *50 Psychology Classics,* 2nd edition, Nicholas Brealey Publishing, London (2017).

Carter P, *IQ and Psychometric Tests* 2nd edn, Kogan Page, London (2007).

Cateora, PR, *International Marketing,* 9th edn, Irwin, Chicago (1996).

Cipolla, CM, *The Economic History of World Population,* 6th edn, Penguin, London (1974).

Clark JL, *Mind Magic & Mentalism for Dummies,* Wiley, Chichester UK (2012).

Cole, Brent (with Dale Carnegie & Associates), *How To Win Friends & Influence People in The Digital Age,* Simon & Schuster, New York (2011).

Cooke T, ed., *Concise History of World Religions,* National Geographic, Washington DC (2011).

REFERENCES

Cozolino L, *The Neuroscience of Psychotherapy, Building and Rebuilding the Human Brain,* W.W. Norton & Co., NY (2002).

Davies, D, *An Introduction to Clinical Psychiatry,* Melbourne University Press, Melbourne (1971).

Dawkins R, *The God Delusion*, Mariner/Houghton Mifflin, Boston (2008).

Dawood NF (translator), *The Koran,* 50th anniversary edition, Penguin, London (2006).

De Bono E, *Lateral Thinking for Management,* Pelican, Harmondsworth (1982).

Eagly AH, Chaiken S, *The Psychology of Attitudes,* Harcourt Brace Jovanovich, Orlando FL (1993).

Egerton Eastwick RW (ed.), *The Oracle Encyclopaedia,* George Newnes, London (1896).

Encarta Encyclopedia 1999, Microsoft Corporation, 1998.

Fancher RE, *The intelligence men: Makers of the IQ Controversy,* WW Norton, New York (1985).

Forbes HD, *Ethnic Conflict: Commerce, Culture, and the Contact Hypothesis,* Yale University Press, New Haven (1997).

Galton D, *In Our Own Image, Eugenics and the Genetic Modification of People*, Little Brown & Co, London (2001).

Gardner L, *Bloodline of the Holy Grail, The Hidden Lineage of Jesus Revealed,* Penguin, London (2001).

Gillespie, David, *Taming Toxic People, The science of identifying & dealing with psychopaths at work & at home,* Pan MacMillan Australia, Sydney (2017).

Goodall (van Lawick-Goodall), Jane, *In the Shadow of Man*, Houghton Mifflin, Boston (1971).

Govoni N, Eng R, Morton G, *Promotional Management: Issues and Perspectives,* Prentice-Hall, Englewood Cliffs NJ (1988).

174

REFERENCES

Hawkins Doug, *Hawk Manure, Funny Footy Yarns, etc.,* Celebrity Books, Melbourne (1995).

Krapp K, editor, *Psychologists & Their Theories for Students,* vol. 1: A-K, Thomson Gale, Farmington Hills, MI (2005).

Larsen RJ, Buss DM, *Personality Psychology, Domains of Knowledge About Human Nature,* McGraw-Hill, NY (2002).

Lieberman JA, *Shrinks, The Untold Story of Psychiatry,* Little Brown & Co, NY (2015).

Likert R, *New Patterns of Management,* McGraw-Hill, New York (1961).

Lilienfeld SO, Lynne SJ, Ruscia J, Beyerstein BL, *50 Great Myths of Popular Psychology, Shattering Widespread Misconceptions about Human Behaviour,* Wiley-Blackwell, Chichester (2010).

Lopez. Shane J., *Making Hope Happen, Create The Future You Want for Yourself and Others,* Atria, New York (2013).

Lindzey G, Hall CS, Thompson RF, *Psychology,* 2nd edn, Worth, New York (1978).

Marta, Suzy Yehl, *Healing the Hurt, Restoring the Hope,* Rodale, London (2004).

McCormack MH, *What They Don't Teach You at Harvard Business School,* Fontana/Collins, London (1986).

McGuire WJ, A syllogistic analysis of cognitive relationships, in *Attitude Organization And Change,* CI Hovland and MJ Rosenberg (eds.), Yale University Press, New Haven (1960).

Meadows DH, Meadows DL, Randers J, Behrens WW, *The Limits to Growth,* Pan, London (1974).

Miller, Nick, 'New hope of escaping the dark', *The Age,* 26 August, 2017.

Mohr GA, Milner HR, *A Microcomputer Introduction to The Finite Element Method,* Pitman, Melbourne (1986), Heinemann, London (1987).

Mohr GA, *Finite Elements for Solids, Fluids, and Optimization,* Oxford University Press, OUP Oxford (1992).

Mohr GA, *Mohr's Laws, What Went Wrong With You and the World and What To Do About It,* Independent Publishers Limited, Mohr (2003).

Mohr GA, *The Pretentious Persuaders, A Brief History & Science of Mass Persuasion,* Horizon Publishing Group, Sydney (2012a).

Mohr GA, *The Doomsday Calculation: The End of the Human Race,* Xlibris, Sydney (2012b).

Mohr GA, *The Variant Virus: Introducing Secret Agent Simon Sinclair,* Xlibris, Sydney (2012c).

Mohr GA, *The War of the Sexes: Women Are Getting On Top,* Xlibris, Sydney (2012d).

Mohr GA, *The History & Psychology of Human Conflict,* Horizon Publishing Group, Sydney (2014a).

Mohr GA, *Elementary Thinking For The 21st Century,* Xlibris, Sydney (2014b).

Mohr GA, *The Pretentious Persuaders, A Brief History & Science of Mass Persuasion,* 2nd edition, Horizon Publishing Group, Sydney (2014c).

Mohr GA, Sinclair R, Fear E, *The Evolving Universe, Relativity, Redshift, and Life From Space,* Xlibris, Sydney (2014).

Mohr GA, Fear E, *World Religions, The History, Issues, & Truth,* Xlibris, Sydney (2015).

Mohr GA, Fear E, Sinclair R, *World War 3: When & How Will It End?,* Inspiring Publishers, Canberra (2015).

Mohr GA, Fear E, *The Brainwashed: From Consumer Zombies to Islamism & Jihad,* Inspiring Publishers, Canberra (2016).

Mohr GA, Sinclair R, Fear E, *Human Intelligence, Learning & Behaviour,* Inspiring Publishers, Canberra (2017).

Mohr GA, *The Scientific MBA,* Balboa Press, Bloomington IN (2017).

Morgan CT, King RA, Robinson NM, *Introduction to Psychology,* 6th edn, McGraw-Hill, Tokyo (1979).

Newcomb TM, Persistence and regression of changed attitudes, *Journal of Sociological Issues* 19 (1963) 3-14.

O'Guinn TC, Allen CT, Semenik RJ, *Advertising and Integrated Brand Promotion.* Thomson South-Western, Mason OH 2006.

Ostrander S, Schroeder L, *Superlearning,* Delacorte Press/Confucian Press, New York (1979).

Packard V, *The Waste Makers,* Pelican, Harmondsworth, London (1963).

Packard V, *The People Shapers,* Nelson, Melbourne (1978).

Parkinson CN, *The Law,* Schwartz, Melbourne (1980).

Penn, *Microtrends, The Small Forces Behind Today's Big Changes*, Allen Lane, London (2007).

Peter LJ, Hull R, *The Peter Principle,* Souvenir Press, London (1969).

Robertson I, *Sociology*, 2nd edn, Worth, New York (1981).

Sampson A, *The Arms Bazaar,* Coronet Books, London (1977).

Snyder, CR, *The Psychology of Hope, You Can Get Here From There,* Simon & Schuster, New York, NY (1994).

Solomon MR, *Consumer Behaviour: Buying, Having and Being,* Allyn and Bacon, Boston (1992).

Sweeney MS, *Brain, The Complete Mind, How it Develops, How it Works, and How to Keep it Sharp,* National Geographic, Washington D.C. (2009).

Sykes CJ, *Dumbing Down Our Kids: Why American Children Feel Good About Themselves But Can't Read, Write or Add*, St Martin's Griffin, New York (1995).

Thomas M, *As Used on the Famous Nelson Mandela, Underground Adventures in the Arms and Torture Trade*, Ebury Press, London (2006).

Thomas J, Hughes T, *You Don't Have to be Famous to Have Manic Depression: The Insider's Guide to Mental Health*, Michael Joseph, London (2006).

Trump, Donald, *The Way to the Top, The Best Business Advice I Ever Received*, Crown Business, New York, NY (2004).

Vernon PE, *Intelligence and Attainment Tests*, University of London Press, London (1960).

Weiss ML, Mann AE, *Human Biology and Behaviour, An Anthropological Perspective*, 2nd edn, Little Brown, Boston MA (1978).

Wolfe L, Americans Target Of Largest Media Brainwashing Campaign In History. Posted on the Internet and originally in *Executive Intelligence Review*, 16/10/01.

Youngson RM, Schott I, *Medical Blunders*, Robinson, London (1996).

REFERENCES

THE PSYCHOLOGY OF HOPE

Hope, optimism and positivity can play an important role in making our lives, and the lives of others much better.

Some of the main topics discussed in this book include:

➢ The importance of encouragement and hope for the young.
➢ How religions were invented and gave us false hope.
➢ Hope improves health, life and longevity.
➢ How positive leadership improves workplace productivity.
➢ How advertising and propaganda 'brainwash' us.
➢ The psychology of attitudes and attitude measurement.
➢ The wide range of psychological disorders.
➢ The psychology of habits.
➢ Contact hypothesis and an attitudinal model of conflict.
➢ Treatments for psychological problems.
➢ Building self-confidence, hope, and self-reliance.
➢ Planning a successful life.
➢ Dealing with bad and psychopathic bosses.
➢ Measuring and improving the quality of one's life.
➢ The 10 laws of a new religion.

G.A. Mohr did his PhD in Churchill College, Cambridge
He published 50 international papers & more than 20 books, including:

➢ *A Microcomputer Introduction to the Finite Element Method*
➢ *Finite Elements for Solids, Fluids, and Optimization*
➢ *Curing Cancer & Heart Disease*
➢ *Heart Disease, Cancer and Ageing*
➢ *The Pretentious Persuaders*
➢ *The War of the Sexes*
➢ *The Variant Virus*
➢ *The Doomsday Calculation*
➢ *2045: A Remote Town Survives Global Holocaust*
➢ *The History and Psychology of Human Conflicts*
➢ *Elementary Thinking for the 21st Century*
➢ *The 8 Week+ Cure for Cardiovascular Disease*
➢ *The Scientific MBA*

and co-authored with Richard Sinclair & Edwin Fear
(nom de plumes for R. S. Mohr and P. E. Mohr)

➢ *World Religions*
➢ *The Brainwashed*
➢ *World War 3*
➢ *Human Intelligence, Learning & Behaviour*
➢ *The Evolving Universe: Relativity, Redshift & Life from Space.*

Printed in the United States
By Bookmasters